Cambridge Elements ≡

Elements in Philosophy of Science
edited by
Jacob Stegenga
University of Cambridge

ABDUCTIVE REASONING
IN SCIENCE

Finnur Dellsén
*University of Iceland, Inland Norway University of
Applied Sciences and University of Oslo*

CAMBRIDGE
UNIVERSITY PRESS

Shaftesbury Road, Cambridge CB2 8EA, United Kingdom

One Liberty Plaza, 20th Floor, New York, NY 10006, USA

477 Williamstown Road, Port Melbourne, VIC 3207, Australia

314–321, 3rd Floor, Plot 3, Splendor Forum, Jasola District Centre, New Delhi – 110025, India

103 Penang Road, #05–06/07, Visioncrest Commercial, Singapore 238467

Cambridge University Press is part of Cambridge University Press & Assessment, a department of the University of Cambridge.

We share the University's mission to contribute to society through the pursuit of education, learning and research at the highest international levels of excellence.

www.cambridge.org
Information on this title: www.cambridge.org/9781009500524

DOI: 10.1017/9781009353199

First published 2024

A catalogue record for this publication is available from the British Library.

ISBN 978-1-009-50052-4 Hardback
ISBN 978-1-009-35318-2 Paperback
ISSN 2517-7273 (online)
ISSN 2517-7265 (print)

Abductive Reasoning in Science

Elements in Philosophy of Science

DOI: 10.1017/9781009353199
First published online: June 2024

Finnur Dellsén
University of Iceland, Inland Norway University of Applied Sciences and University of Oslo

Author for correspondence: Finnur Dellsén, fud@hi.is

Abstract: In *abductive reasoning*, scientific theories are evaluated on the basis of how well they would explain the available evidence. There are a number of subtly different accounts of this type of reasoning, most of which are inspired by the popular slogan "Inference to the Best Explanation." However, these accounts disagree about exactly how to spell out the slogan so as to avoid various problems for abductive reasoning. This Element aims, firstly, to give an opinionated overview both of the many accounts of abductive reasoning that have been proposed and the problems that have motivated them; and, secondly, to critically evaluate these accounts in a way that points toward a systematic view of the nature and purpose of abductive reasoning in science. This title is also available as Open Access on Cambridge Core.

Keywords: abduction, inference to the best explanation, scientific reasoning, explanatory virtues, alternative explanations

ISBNs: 9781009500524 (HB), 9781009353182 (PB), 9781009353199 (OC)
ISSNs: 2517-7273 (online), 2517-7265 (print)

Contents

Introduction

Scientists are constantly engaged in various forms of reasoning, arguing that because *this* is the case, *that* must be the case. Some of these forms of reasoning are from what may broadly be called *data* to what may broadly be called *theory*. The data are things like observations, survey statistics, and experimental results. A theory is typically a more ambitious type of claim that often generalizes, expands, or otherwise "goes beyond" the data, such as by specifying what causes some type of event. For example, by the early twentieth century there was already a great deal of observational data suggesting that lung cancer is more frequent among tobacco smokers than among non-smokers. From this data most scientists eventually inferred that smoking *causes* lung cancer, and so that one may reduce one's chances of getting lung cancer by refraining from smoking.

The term "abductive reasoning" refers, at least for the purposes of this *Element*, to a specific way of engaging in data-to-theory reasoning. In particular, it refers to reasoning in which theories are evaluated at least partly on the basis of how well they would, if true, *explain* the available data. To see how this is supposed to work, consider how one might conclude that smoking causes lung cancer in the above example. The theory that smoking causes lung cancer seems to provide a good explanation, especially compared to rival explanations, of the observed difference in lung cancer frequency among smokers and nonsmokers. In particular, the theory that smoking causes lung cancer arguably provides a much better explanation of this data than various other theories one might think of, such as that the correlation between smoking and lung cancer is a mere coincidence, or that having lung cancer somehow causes smoking.[1] On these grounds, it seems reasonable to conclude that smoking causes lung cancer.

Abductive reasoning is arguably not only commonplace in the sciences, but also widespread in other situations in which we make inferences about the underlying explanations, such as the causes or grounds, of the things in our immediate environment. Some philosophers even claim that all cogent data-to-theory reasoning is abductive reasoning – that is, that reasoning from data to theory should always involve evaluating how well various theories would explain the data (e.g., Lycan, 1988). According to this view, even the most basic generalizations and predictions from past experience – such as inferring that the sun will rise tomorrow morning because it has risen every morning thus far – involve abductive reasoning as well, albeit in an implicit and indirect

---

[1] This latter type of explanation was seriously proposed by R.A. Fisher (1959), who suggested that having lung cancer might cause an unconscious irritation or pain, which in turn causes people to smoke.

way. Furthermore, several philosophers have argued that abductive reasoning is essential to philosophy itself – that philosophical theories should be evaluated on the basis of how well they explain some philosophical "data," such as our pre-theoretic judgments about hypothetical cases (e.g., Williamson, 2016).

Given the apparent significance of abductive reasoning, it should come as no surprise that philosophers of science have studied the nature of abductive reasoning intensely. In the past few decades, a number of subtly different accounts of abductive reasoning have emerged – many, though not all, of which have been inspired by Gilbert Harman's (1965) slogan "Inference to the Best Explanation." Roughly, Harman's idea was that one may infer a theory from some collection of data just in case the theory provides a better explanation of the data than any competing theory that one has considered, where inference involves coming to accept or believe that the theory is true. However, the popularity of Harman's slogan obscures how much disagreement there is about exactly how to understand it. A number of very serious, if not devastating, objections have prompted various philosophers to reconsider key elements of the slogan. Indeed, there are now prominent accounts on which Inference to the Best Explanation is not viewed as a form of *inference*, some accounts on which it does not involve inferring to the *best* explanation, and yet others on which one need not infer to an *explanation* at all.[2]

This Element has two main aims. The first is to give a systematic and opinionated overview of the current state of philosophical thinking about abductive reasoning. This involves not just discussing the various accounts of abductive reasoning that have been proposed, but also the many objections to previous accounts which have motivated philosophers to develop them. As this indicates, I will approach the topic in a problem-based manner, in the sense that the various accounts of abductive reasoning will be presented as responses to specific problems. However, some problems and accounts will not be discussed in detail, or indeed at all. This is partly for reasons of space and partly to keep the discussion accessible, since some important contributions to the topic are rather technical and require familiarity with various formal methods that would need to be introduced in an Element of their own.[3]

The second aim of this Element is to gradually construct, by drawing lessons from the various problems and accounts to be discussed, a systematic view of

---

[2] This curious situation evokes Voltaire's (1759, ch. 70) quip that the Holy Roman Empire was "in no way holy, nor Roman, nor an empire."

[3] Happily, there is another Element, *Bayesianism and Scientific Reasoning* (Schupbach, 2022), that covers much of the ground I have in mind here, especially recent discussions of formal measures of explanatory power and how they could be leveraged in an account of abductive reasoning.

the nature and purpose of abductive reasoning. This view is difficult to summarize briefly at this stage, but at a very general level it holds that abductive reasoning is a collection of inferential strategies that serves to approximate different forms of probabilistic reasoning. Depending on the exact nature of the probabilistic reasoning that is being approximated, the inferential strategy may be more or less demanding. In particular, I will suggest that some of the probabilistic conclusions we wish to reach are quite modest, for example, when determining which theory to investigate further; in those cases, abductive reasoning is not very demanding. In other cases, we may want abductive reasoning to warrant a reasonably high level of probabilistic confidence that a theory is true; in those cases, abductive reasoning is an evidentially demanding and temporally extended process that may not deliver the desired conclusion at all.

The rest of this Element is structured as follows. Section 1 briefly summarizes the history of philosophical thought about abductive reasoning from the advent of modern science to the middle of the twentieth century. Section 2 surveys contemporary accounts of abductive reasoning, based on a three-fold distinction between accounts that construe abductive reasoning as (i) a form of *inference*, (ii) a *probabilistic* process, or (iii) *both* of the above. Section 3 focuses on the fact that in abductive reasoning, one is told to infer or prefer the *best* explanation. But what reason, if any, is there for scientists to prefer "better" explanations in this way? As we shall see, there are several quite different types of answers to this question, leading to different ideas about the role of abductive reasoning in science. Section 4 then discusses a different set of problems for accounts of abductive reasoning, having to do with whether abductive reasoning is somehow irrational or incoherent in some cases. In particular, it has been suggested that some common accounts of abductive reasoning imply that one should sometimes infer theories that are, by one's own lights, very likely to be false; or that one should assign probabilities to theories in ways that are, by one's own lights, demonstrably irrational. Finally, Section 5 weaves together various threads from the previous sections to briefly present a holistic view of abductive reasoning that, I hope, avoids the various problems for abductive reasoning discussed in this Element while retaining the core insight that much of scientific reasoning is governed by explanatory considerations.

1 A Brief History of Abductive Reasoning

This section introduces the topic of this Element by way of a brief historical overview of philosophical thinking about abductive reasoning. In particular, we will look at examples of scientists and philosophers who deployed or implicitly endorsed forms of abductive reasoning, such as Charles Darwin and René

Descartes (§1.1); discuss Charles S. Peirce's pioneering work on the form of reasoning he dubbed "Abduction" (§1.2); consider the extent to which the "hypothetico-deductive model" is a forerunner to abductive reasoning (§1.3); and, finally, examine Gilbert Harman's seminal notion of "Inference to the Best Explanation" (§1.4). This overview sets the stage for the next section, in which more recent (and arguably more sophisticated) accounts of abductive reasoning are surveyed.

1.1 The Historical Roots of Abductive Reasoning

As is so often the case with methodological novelties, abductive reasoning seems to have emerged first as an implicit scientific practice rather than an explicit philosophical theory. This is perhaps clearest in the writings of Francis Bacon (1561–1626), often regarded as the father of "the scientific method." Rebelling against the Aristotelian idea that natural philosophy (i.e., science) can discover the essences of things, Bacon explicitly advocated an austere form of "inductivism" in his influential *Novum Organum* (Bacon, 1620). According to Bacon, scientists should proceed by first collecting data, for example, by observing that this or that pot of water boils at 100°C. Having collected such data, they should then generalize from observed correlations in that data, for example, by concluding that water *always* boils at 100°C. In short, Bacon's official view identified scientific reasoning with extrapolation from data.

In practice, however, Bacon seems to have allowed for a different type of reasoning to play an important role in science (McMullin, 1992, 175–179). Bacon was an early advocate of what was later dubbed the kinetic theory of heat, which holds that heat can be identified with the motion of unobservably small parts of the heated body (i.e., what we would now call *molecules*). But how could Bacon establish that these unobservably small parts move around within the heated body in the first place, or indeed that they exist at all? Baconian generalization from a correlation among observations cannot do the trick, since there was never a correlation to generalize; there is no correlation between observations of hot bodies and observations of bodies consisting of small parts in motion, simply because those parts are hypothesized to be too small to see. So, in his scientific practice, Bacon seems to have been relying on some additional form of reasoning in which we are given license to postulate the existence of unobservable entities to explain observable phenomena, such as heat.

Something similar can be said of René Descartes (1596–1650). In contrast to Bacon the empiricist, Descartes the rationalist held that scientific knowledge (*scientia*) is grounded in the "simple natures" of objects, which we can come to know through direct apprehension, or "intuition." In his influential methodological essay, *Rules for the Direction of the Mind* (1985/1628), Descartes repeatedly warns against settling for "merely probable cognition," instead urging us to "resolve to believe only what is perfectly known and incapable of being doubted" (Descartes, 1985/1628, 10). This may seem to leave little room for abductive reasoning – which, after all, uses empirical data rather than direct apprehensions into simple natures, and delivers theories that are very much capable of being doubted.

However, a closer look at Descartes's own scientific writings, especially in his later work *Principles of Philosophy* (1985/1644), paints a more nuanced picture. Accompanying Descartes's official rationalist theory of scientific reasoning, scholars have found an implicit scientific methodology that resembles abductive reasoning in some important respects (Clarke, 1992; Dellsén, 2017b). In more than 300 separate sections, Descartes posits various novel and ingenious mechanisms to explain numerous natural phenomena, such as why bodies fall toward the earth, how magnets work, and why glass is transparent. Descartes prefaces the discussion by telling us that he wishes to "put forward everything that I am about to write simply as a hypothesis," adding in the French edition that it "is perhaps far from the truth" (Descartes, 1985/1644, 255). Clearly, then, Descartes felt the need to employ some other form of reasoning – in which hypotheses are fallibly posited to explain known phenomena – in addition to his official rationalist and infallibilist methodology.

The methodological necessity of some form of abductive reasoning is also apparent in the writings of various prominent scientists of the early modern period (Thagard, 1978). For example, Antoine Lavoisier's (1743–1794) work on chemical phenomena such as combustion and calcination led him to posit the existence of oxygen, because with it "all the phenomena were explained with an astonishing simplicity" (Lavoisier, 1862, 623). Similarly, Charles Darwin ends his famous discussion of a vast range of empirical facts about biological species that support his theory of evolution by writing: "It can hardly be supposed that a false theory could explain, in so satisfactory a manner as does the theory of natural selection, the several large classes of facts above specified" (Darwin, 1962, 476). Darwin explicitly defended his use of this "method of arguing" by pointing out that "it is a method used in judgment of the common events of life, and has often been used by the greatest natural philosophers" (Darwin, 1962, 476).

In sum, then, it appears that something like abductive reasoning – in which theories are posited to explain known phenomena – emerged during the advent of modern science amongst scientific luminaries such as Bacon, Descartes, Lavoisier, and Darwin. However, as noted above, this form of reasoning appears to have been largely implicit amongst working scientists of this period, rather than being based on an explicit account of how reasoning of this kind ought to proceed.

1.2 Peirce's Notion of "Abduction"

This began to change with the work of the American pragmatist Charles S. Peirce (1839–1914), from whom the term "abduction" and its cognates seem to originate. Peirce wrote a number of works touching on the topic over his long career, often contrasting "Abduction" with both "Deduction" and "Induction." In one frequently quoted passage, Peirce (1958, 5.145) writes that Abduction follows the following schema:

> The surprising fact C is observed.
> But if A were true, C would be a matter of course.
> Hence, there is reason to suspect that A is true.

For example, one may notice the surprising fact that a burning object placed in a vacuum immediately stops burning. If, as Lavoisier claimed, combustion is a process in which a burning substance combines with oxygen, then this surprising fact would be a matter of course. Hence, according to Peirce's Abduction schema, there is reason to suspect that Lavoisier's theory is true.

It is worth noting that Peirce was arguably not entirely consistent over time about how he defined 'Abduction' – or, indeed, regarding which term he used for it, preferring "Hypothesis" and "Retroduction" in his earlier work. Moreover, most contemporary readers of Peirce agree that his use of the term "Abduction" differs in important ways from how the term tends to be used and understood today. In particular, several scholars (Hanson, 1958; Kapitan, 1992; Minnameier, 2004; Campos, 2011) have argued that in his most influential works, Peirce uses "Abduction" to refer to a psychological process of generating or suggesting new hypotheses. Put differently, the standard interpretation of Peirce's work is that his notion of Abduction primarily describes the process by which we can or should come to think of novel theories, namely by considering what type of theory would potentially explain the facts before us, regardless of whether those theories can be considered true or plausible.

Apart from textual evidence supporting this interpretation, there are philosophical reasons for taking Peircean Abduction to be something other than a rule of inference – or, at most, to be a very weak rule of inference. After all, it should be clear that the same set of facts may lead, via a Peircean Abduction, to quite different, indeed incompatible, theories. Put in terms of the above schema, for each C there will arguably be several incompatible theories $A_1, \ldots, A_n$ such that if each A_i were true, then C would be "a matter of course." For example, note that Lavoisier's oxygen theory of combustion is not the only theory on which we should expect an object to stop burning once placed in a vacuum. Consider instead the theory that burning involves the transfer of a specific substance, phlogiston, from the object to the surrounding air. This theory also explains why nothing burns in a vacuum, because in a vacuum there is no air to receive the phlogiston that would otherwise be transferred from the object. So which theory, Lavoisier's oxygen-based theory or this phlogiston-based theory, should be inferred? (We cannot infer both, since the two theories contradict each other.) Peircean Abduction, by itself, does not answer these questions, which in turn suggests that Peirce did not intend it to be a rule of inference at all.

A note on terminology is appropriate at this point. As I have intimated, contemporary authors usually use the term "abduction" to refer to an epistemic process of providing support for explanatory hypotheses (see, e.g., Douven, 2021). This is a process that is meant to make certain theories plausible or believable, as opposed to merely helping us come up with those theories. In order to prevent confusion between Peirce's notion of Abduction and the contemporary notion of abduction, I have chosen to use the term "abductive reasoning" when referring to the latter; and, on those occasions I refer to the former, I will use "generation of explanatory hypotheses." Keeping these notions clearly distinct from one another is important for a number of reasons. For example, some accounts of abductive reasoning (e.g., Lipton, 2004) take it to involve, as one part of the process, the generation of explanatory hypotheses (see §2.2).

1.3 The Hypothetico-Deductive Model

Peirce's notion of Abduction is an important early precursor to contemporary accounts of abductive reasoning. Another idea that is arguably just as important a precursor to such accounts is the so-called *hypothetico-deductive model* (the HD model; also known as the hypothetico-deductive *method*), often associated with William Whewell, Hans Reichenbach, and Carl G. Hempel, among others.[4]

---

[4] See, for example, Sankey (2008, 251) and Okasha and Thébault (2020, 774). With that said, as far as I know, none of the authors mentioned above advocate the simple version of the HD model described below. Of the three, Hempel is perhaps the one that comes closest to doing so in his textbook *The Philosophy of Natural Science* (Hempel, 1966, 196–199). However, a discussion in a textbook can hardly be assumed to accurately reflect Hempel's own considered views on the topic. Indeed, Hempel (1945) proposes a much more nuanced theory of confirmation that conflicts in important ways with the HD model (on this, see Crupi, 2021, §2.1).

The HD model can be thought of as a combination of two ideas. The first idea is about the temporal priority of theory over data. The HD model says, in direct opposition to the inductivism of Francis Bacon, that one should formulate one's theory before one starts gathering data (e.g., by making observations and doing experiments). In other words, one should start by "hypothesizing." At this point, the theory is merely a guess, a hypothesis; it is not something the theorist must take to be true, probably true, or even particularly plausible. According to Hempel (1966, 201–207) there are no rules of rationality for how one should go about coming up with such hypotheses – one may simply let one's imagination roam free in search of some guess that might work. Indeed, it would be impossible to formulate such rules, according to Hempel, because oftentimes the correct guess will be completely different from one's earlier way of approaching the issue, and also very different from the empirical data one has gathered so far. In particular, the guess might well postulate the existence of some new type of entity that cannot be directly observed at all, such as subatomic particles or electromagnetic fields.

The other part of the HD model concerns how this guess – this hypothesis – is evaluated. According to the HD model, the hypothesis is evaluated by testing its empirical consequences. An empirical consequence of a hypothesis is something that can be deduced from it, given background assumptions, and that can be directly verified in some way, such as by an observation or experiment. If these empirical consequences are shown to be correct, the theory from which they have been deduced is confirmed or supported according to the HD model. So the logical structure of scientific confirmation, according to the HD model, is as follows:

The HD model (scientific confirmation): A theory T is confirmed (to some extent), given some background assumptions $\mathcal{A}$, just in case:

(i) T, together with $\mathcal{A}$, deductively implies an empirical consequence E; and

(ii) E is indeed correct, as shown by empirical data.

We are now in a position to see why the HD model has the word "deductive" in it. It's because, in order for the theory to be supported by the observations or experimental results, the empirical consequences which serve as evidence for the theory must be *deducible* from the theory. However, note that what is being deduced is not the theory itself; rather, it is the empirical consequences of the theory. And yet it is the theory that is being supported or confirmed, not (just) its empirical consequences.

There is a caveat to the HD model as presented above that will prove to be important as we contrast it below with prominent accounts of abductive reasoning. It's that on this presentation of the HD model, it is not a model of how to end up with a theory that we can infer or accept, all things considered. Rather, the HD model may only describe what it is for a theory T to gain some degree of confirmation from a set of empirical data, which may only consist in making T somewhat more credible than it would otherwise have been. After all, verifying a single empirical consequence of some theory surely does not by itself show that the theory is true, or even probably true. Some authors suggest that this issue can be addressed by slightly modifying the HD model by requiring a greater number of T's empirical consequences to be verified, at which point T may be inferred to be true:

The HD model (scientific inference): A theory T may be inferred to be true, given some background assumptions $\mathcal{A}$, just in case:

(i) T, together with $\mathcal{A}$, deductively implies some empirical consequences $E_1, \ldots, E_m$; and

(ii) $E_1, \ldots, E_m$ are indeed correct, as shown by empirical data.

Now, there are clearly some important similarities between the Peirce's notion of Abduction, on the one hand, and the HD model of scientific confirmation and inference, on the other. In particular, the structures of the two types of accounts are remarkably similar: both require a kind of derivation of a manifest fact from a hypothetical guess. The most important difference concerns the fact that, as we have noted, Peirce appears to be concerned with the process of generating theories rather than with how theories should be evaluated. By contrast, Hempel explicitly leaves this out of his HD model, on the grounds that there can be no rational rules for generating new theories. In this respect, Hempel's HD model and Peircean Abduction are diametrically opposed ideas. This makes it especially interesting, and frankly somewhat puzzling, that the structures of the accounts are so similar, since one would not expect accounts of two quite different aspects of scientific methodology to end up being structurally so similar to one another.

Indeed, the similarity in structure between Peircean Abduction and the HD model points to a well-known problem for the latter that will be familiar from our earlier discussion of the former. Recall that in a Peircean Abduction, for each "surprising fact" C there will arguably be several incompatible propositions $A_1, \ldots, A_n$ such that if each A_i were true, then C would be "a matter of course." A similar point applies to the HD model as applied to scientific confirmation: For each empirical consequence E, there will inevitably be several theories $T_1, \ldots, T_n$ from which E may be deduced. This point may be illustrated by returning to the example of Lavoisier's oxygen theory of combustion, which arguably implies the empirical fact that nothing burns in a vacuum. The problem is that the competing phlogiston theory, at least as formulated above, implies the very same empirical fact. Thus, the HD model must say that *both* theories are confirmed; moreover, the model has no resources to say that one of the two theories is confirmed to a greater extent than the other. The same goes for any other theory from which this empirical fact can be deduced, however implausible it might seem in other respects.

One might think that this is less of a problem for the HD model as applied to scientific *inference*, given that it involves deducing not a single empirical consequence E but a set of such consequences $E_1, \ldots, E_m$, all of which have been shown to be correct by empirical data. After all, the thought might go, although it would be easy to come up with a theory that entails a single E, it need not be so easy to come up with a theory that entails all of $E_1, \ldots, E_m$ (provided that m is a sufficiently large number). Unfortunately, however, given a single theory T that implies $E_1, \ldots, E_m$, it is quite easy to use elementary logic to come up with another theory that does so as well. For example, it's a logical fact that if T implies $E_1, \ldots, E_m$, then so does the conjunction T&X, where X can be any claim whatsoever. Indeed, any set of empirical claims $E_1, \ldots, E_m$ is trivially implied by the conjunction of those claims and any other claim X, that is, by $E_1 \& \ldots \& E_m \& X$. Here, X could be a claim that contradicts T, such as the negation of T, ¬T. This leaves us with the absurd conclusion that the HD model allows one to infer T and a claim that directly contradicts T, namely $E_1 \& \ldots \& E_m \& \neg T$.

Something has clearly gone quite wrong in the HD model. The solution might seem obvious. For surely the issue here is that the alternative "theories" that imply our empirical data $E_1, \ldots, E_m$ are highly artificial, or just plain implausible – so much so that no actual scientists would propose such theories with a straight face. This is correct, but it's not so much a solution to the problem as it is the beginnings of a diagnosis of it. In order to solve the problem, we need an account of scientific reasoning in which artificial or implausible "theories" are not so easily confirmable or inferable by empirical data. If possible, the account should also be able to *explain why* this is the case. Unfortunately for the HD model, it fails to do either of these things. As we shall see below, however, some accounts of abductive reasoning do significantly better on this score. Hence abductive reasoning, or at least some accounts thereof, can be viewed as improvements on the HD model in this respect.

Before we move on, it is worth noting another problem for the HD model of scientific confirmation and inference. This problem concerns the "deductive" part of the HD model, that is, the requirement that it must be possible to *deduce* correct empirical claims from the theory that is being confirmed or inferred. In short, the problem is that many scientific theories, especially those that concern causal relationships between two or more variables, do not categorically state that a given event will definitively occur under specified circumstances; rather, these theories often only state that the event has a particular chance of occurring in those circumstances. Indeed, sometimes the probability of this chance event is extremely low. Consider, for example, the geological theories that are used to predict when and where earthquakes will occur, which might assign a 0.1% probability to an earthquake occurring during a given week in a very high-risk area. In these cases, there is no deductive relationship between theory and empirical data, because for each piece of data (e.g., for each earthquake that is observed to occur), it is perfectly possible – perhaps even probable – that one would have obtained contrary data (e.g., an observation that no earthquake occurred) even if the relevant theory is true.

Probabilistic theories of this sort are problematic for the HD model because although we cannot *deduce* any empirical consequences from the theories, it nevertheless seems clear that empirical results can confirm them. For example, suppose that a newly proposed geological theory implies that the probability of an earthquake in your city sometime next week is as high as 10%, whereas all other available theories assign a less than 0.00001% probability to this event. If the earthquake subsequently occurs, then surely the new theory can be considered confirmed to some extent, at least relative to its rivals. And if a similar story were to repeat itself in other geographical areas and at other times, with the new theory assigning a much higher probability to earthquakes that actually occur, then at some point we may feel that the theory ought to be believed or accepted as true. Unfortunately for the HD model, it cannot deliver these verdicts, for none of the theories involved implies that the earthquake will occur, only that it has some probability of occurring.

In sum, then, we have seen that the HD model faces at least two serious problems. The first concerns how to discriminate between the "serious" theories that are confirmed by their empirical consequences and various "unserious" theories that are not, such as conjunctions of the empirical consequences themselves and random other claims. The second concerns inherently probabilistic theories – theories from which empirical consequences cannot be deduced but are rather assigned a particular probability. I have focused on these problems here because, as we shall see, even early accounts of abductive reasoning arguably have the resources to address both of these problems. Moreover, these accounts of abductive reasoning often preserve some of the structure of the HD model, and thus are plausibly in a position to account for the kernel of truth in the HD model – which, after all, has seemed to many to provide a fairly accurate description of scientists' actual methodology.[5]

1.4 Inference to the Best Explanation

In 1965, Gilbert Harman published a short paper which has had an enormous influence on philosophical thinking about abductive reasoning ever since. The paper was entitled "The Inference to the Best Explanation." This term, standardly abbreviated to "IBE," is now often used for any type or account of abductive reasoning.[6] Harman acknowledged that his notion of IBE "corresponds approximately" to earlier ideas about scientific reasoning, such as "abduction" and "the method of hypothesis," but used his own terminology to "avoid most of the misleading suggestions of alternative terminologies" (Harman, 1965, 88–89). Harman thus goes on to briefly describe his own notion of IBE in a passage that is worth quoting in full:

> In making this inference one infers, from the fact that a certain hypothesis would explain the evidence, to the truth of that hypothesis. In general, there will be several hypotheses which might explain the evidence, so one must be able to reject all such alternative hypotheses before one is warranted in making the inference. Thus one infers, from the premise that a given hypothesis would provide a "better" explanation for the evidence than would any other hypothesis, to the conclusion that the given hypothesis is true.
>
> There is, of course, a problem about how one is to judge that one hypothesis is sufficiently better than another hypothesis. Presumably such a judgment will be based on considerations such as which hypothesis is simpler, which is more plausible, which explains more, which is less *ad hoc*, and so forth. I do not wish to deny that there is a problem about explaining the exact nature of these considerations; I will not, however, say anything more about this problem (Harman, 1965, 89).

Much of this description should remind us of the ideas about scientific reasoning we have encountered earlier in this section. In particular, we have seen that Darwin, Lavoisier, and Peirce all emphasized the significance of "the fact that a certain hypothesis would explain the evidence" for "the truth of that

---

[5] For example, Lipton (2004, 15) writes that "the hypothetico-deductive model seems genuinely to reflect scientific practice, which is perhaps why it has become the scientists' philosophy of science."

[6] As we shall see in the next section, however, only some contemporary accounts of abductive reasoning can be said to be developments of Harman's account; other contemporary accounts depart so significantly from Harman's ideas that they are more fruitfully viewed as competing accounts.

hypothesis." Furthermore, Harman's list of considerations for judging whether one hypothesis is "sufficiently better" than another seem to fit with Lavoisier's and Darwin's remarks, such as those about explaining "several large classes of facts" (Darwin) and doing so "with an astonishing simplicity" (Lavoisier). In Section 3, we will return to these considerations and ask whether Harman (and Lavoisier, Darwin, etc.) was right to think that they make a theory "better" – and, if so, in what sense of that term.

For now, it is worth drawing out some of the more important ways in which Harman's description of IBE differs from most previous ideas about abductive reasoning. First, Harman's IBE is explicitly *comparative*. Despite what Harman seems to be saying at the beginning of the passage, one cannot really infer from the fact that a theory explains the evidence that the theory is true. This is because, as Harman goes on to note, "[i]n general, there will be several hypotheses which might explain the evidence" – and these plainly cannot all be true at the same time. Hence, we get from Harman the more careful statement of IBE as inferring "from the premise that a given hypothesis would provide a "better" explanation for the evidence than would any other hypothesis, to the conclusion that the given hypothesis is true" (Harman, 1965, 89). Inference to the Best Explanation is inference to the best explanatory hypothesis, where "bestness" is a comparative matter of being better than alternative hypotheses.

This comparative aspect of IBE is arguably an improvement over previous and related ideas, such as Peirce's Abduction and the HD model. To see this, consider the first objection to the HD model from the previous subsection (§1.3), according to which the model automatically counts various artificial theories, such as the conjunction $E_1 \& \ldots \& E_m \& X$, for any X, as confirmed by, and inferable from, the evidence $E_1, \ldots, E_m$ which follows (trivially) from it. Harman's IBE, by contrast, does not automatically count such theories as inferable because they might not be – and usually are not – able to provide as good explanations as several alternative theories with which they could be compared. In particular, on an intuitive level at least, such theories will usually be both less simple, and more ad hoc, than several other theories – *less simple* because they will consist of a gerrymandered conjunction of claims; and *more ad hoc* because this conjunction will have been deliberately constructed to contain as conjuncts all the empirical consequences $E_1, \ldots, E_m$.[7]

---

[7] Indeed, in this particular case, it is not clear that a theory like $E_1 \& \ldots \& E_m \& X$ would provide *any* explanation – let alone the *best* explanation – of $E_1, \ldots, E_m$. After all, $E_1 \& \ldots \& E_m \& X$ is a conjunction of $E_1 \& \ldots \& E_m$, which cannot explain itself, and X, which may be completely irrelevant to $E_1 \& \ldots \& E_m$.

Consider also the second objection to the HD model, which concerned inherently probabilistic theories from which empirical consequences cannot be deduced even though the theories assign to them a particular probability. Although Harman himself does not discuss what notion of "explanation" he had in mind, it seems plausible that a theory could explain the occurrence of an event without the event being deducible from the theory. In particular, assigning a reasonably high probability to an event seems to explain that event, at least to some extent and in some cases. Generalizing this point, one might further think that if one theory assigns a higher probability to an event than another theory, then the first theory explains the event more strongly, and thus "better" in one sense of the term, at least all else being equal (Strevens, 2000). And it's natural to think, and certainly in the spirit of Harman's remarks above, that explaining "more strongly," or "better," contributes to making the explanation better overall and thus inferable by a Harman-style IBE.

If so, then it seems that Harman's IBE can account for cases in which inherently probabilistic theories are confirmed by events to which they only assign a probability, and perhaps even a very low probability, provided that the alternative theories assign an even lower probability to those events. To illustrate, consider again the example of a new geological theory on which the occurrence of an earthquake in your city next week is assigned a 0.1% probability while alternative theories all assign a less than 0.00001% probability to this event. If the earthquake subsequently occurs, then the envisioned version of Harman's IBE would count the first theory as providing a much stronger explanation of the earthquake than any of the alternative theories on offer, which in turn would favor inferring the new theory over the alternatives, all else being equal. If a similar story were to repeat itself in other geographical areas and at other times, with the new theory assigning a much higher probability to earthquakes that actually occur, then at some point this might tip the balance in favor of the new geological theory providing the overall best explanation, and thus being inferable by IBE.

In sum, then, Harman's IBE arguably improves on the HD model in both of the two respects in which the HD model falls short. At the same time, Harman's description of this type of inference seems to capture the core insight of the HD model, namely, that much of scientific reasoning involves coming up with educated guesses, in the form of hypotheses or theories, which are then subsequently tested against empirical data. Harman's notion of IBE adds to this (i) that the connection between the theories and the data is explanatory rather than deductive, that is, such that the theory *explains* rather than entails the data; and (ii) that the theories that are inferred or confirmed must provide *better* explanations than other available theories that would also explain the data.

2 Contemporary Accounts of Abductive Reasoning

This section provides an opinionated overview of contemporary accounts of abductive reasoning. We'll start off by distinguishing three types of such accounts: *inferential, probabilistic,* and *hybrid* accounts (§2.1). Inferential accounts construe abductive reasoning as a specific type of inference, in which an explanatory hypothesis is eventually accepted or believed (§2.2). Probabilistic accounts, by contrast, construe abductive reasoning as a form of probabilistic updating that is influenced by explanatory considerations in some way (§2.3). Finally, hybrid accounts construe abduction as a combination of both, in that a distinctively explanatory type of inference serves as a heuristic for approximating some form of probabilistic updating (§2.4).

2.1 A Classification of Accounts

In the previous section, we surveyed part of the history of abductive reasoning and related ideas about scientific reasoning, ending with Harman's notion of Inference to the Best Explanation (IBE). In this section, we pick up the thread in a more recent setting, examining contemporary accounts of abductive reasoning. Some of these accounts owe much to Harman's ideas; others are greatly influenced by earlier thinkers, such as Peirce; and yet others are influenced by the desire to avoid problems with earlier accounts of scientific reasoning, such as the HD model. Thus, we will refer back to the previous section at various points below. From here onwards, however, the discussion will be thematically rather than chronologically organized. To facilitate this discussion, we may classify the different accounts of abductive reasoning that can be found in the contemporary literature into three distinct types:

A first type of accounts may be called *inferential accounts*. These accounts hold that abductive reasoning involves inferring hypotheses on the basis of explanatory considerations, where an *inference* is a type of reasoning in which one draws a categorical conclusion of some type from a set of premises. In particular, these accounts construe abductive reasoning as a type of *ampliative* inference, in which the content of the conclusion goes beyond the content of the premises, and where the premises are constituted by one's evidence at the relevant time. In a typical inferential account of abductive reasoning, it involves *comparing* a number of competing explanatory hypotheses in terms of how good an explanation each would provide us with, and then *accepting* the hypothesis that would provide the best one. As we shall see, inferential accounts are attractive in part because they seem well suited to explaining the actual scientific practice of comparatively evaluating and accepting explanatory hypotheses. Inferential accounts are discussed in Section 2.2.

A second type of accounts may be called *probabilistic accounts*. These accounts hold that abductive reasoning involves assigning probabilities to explanatory hypotheses and updating these probabilities as more evidence is obtained. Thus if one hypothesis explains some piece of incoming data particularly well, whereas another explains the data poorly or not at all, probabilistic accounts say that you should increase the probability assigned to the former at the expense of the probability assigned to the latter. Most probabilistic accounts are amendments or modifications of the Bayesian approach to scientific reasoning, so these accounts take on some of the burdens, but also the benefits, of the Bayesian approach. Probabilistic accounts can deliver impressively precise analyses of how scientists ought to reason under ideal conditions, but they are arguably much less plausible than inferential accounts as descriptions of actual scientific practice. Probabilistic accounts are discussed in Section 2.3.

The third and final type of accounts may be called *hybrid accounts*. These accounts combine elements from each of the other two types of accounts, that is, inferential and probabilistic accounts. While there are important differences between the various hybrid accounts that have been proposed, such accounts generally hold that abductive reasoning involves both a process of generating, comparing, and accepting hypotheses, and also an assignment of probabilities to these hypotheses. In particular, one sort of hybrid account holds that comparing and accepting hypotheses serves as a means to approximate correct probabilistic updating for imperfectly rational agents, such as ordinary humans. If hybrid accounts can be made to work, then they would arguably bring the "best of both worlds" from the other types of accounts, in that they may capture the descriptive accuracy of inferential accounts and the powerful normative framework of probabilistic accounts. Hybrid accounts are discussed in Section 2.4.

As this preliminary overview perhaps indicates, I am myself partial to hybrid accounts. Accordingly, when evaluating the three types of accounts over the course of the current section, I will be gently nudging the reader towards hybrid accounts. However, since hybrid accounts combine elements from both of the other types of accounts, this does not necessarily involve arguing against inferential and probabilistic accounts except in so far as they purport to be the complete story of abductive reasoning. I will, however, present some reasons for preferring some particular accounts of each type as components of a hybrid account of the sort I prefer.

2.2 Inferential Accounts

Recall that what I am calling *inferential accounts* hold that abductive reasoning consists in inferring hypotheses on the basis of explanatory considerations. As noted above, this formulation assumes a quite specific notion of "inference," in which it involves drawing a categorical conclusion of some type from a set of premises. Put more precisely, inference is the mental act of forming a positive epistemic attitude of a non-gradable sort towards some proposition (the conclusion), for example, by accepting, believing, or judging it to be true, because one takes some other propositions (the premises) to provide support for it.[8] So, for example, if one previously suspended judgment on some theory, and thus had no belief either way regarding it, but then one comes to believe that the theory is true as a result of gathering and considering some evidence, then one counts as having inferred the theory from the evidence on this notion of inference. If the inference is moreover based at least partly on explanatory considerations in some way, then it is an instance of abductive reasoning according to inferential accounts thereof.

Many, perhaps most, accounts of abductive reasoning are inferential in this sense.[9] In particular, many of those who follow Harman in thinking of abductive reasoning as IBE seem to be advocating for an inferential account of some sort. For instance, we see proponents of IBE describe it as "accepting a hypothesis on the grounds that it provides a better explanation of the evidence than is provided by alternative hypotheses" (Thagard, 1978, 77), or as "the procedure of choosing the hypothesis or theory that best explains the available data" (Vogel, 2005, 445–446). Indeed, the connection between describing abductive reasoning as IBE, on the one hand, and adhering to some sort of inferential account is natural since Harman himself seems to have been proposing an inferential account when he introduced the term. For Harman, IBE involves ending up with "the conclusion that the given hypothesis is true" (Harman, 1965, 89).[10]

Taking abductive reasoning to be a form of inference still leaves a lot of room for debate about how exactly to best characterize such reasoning in various other respects. To see this, let us consider what is doubtless the most influential account of abductive reasoning since Harman (1965), namely the inferential account presented in Peter Lipton's book *Inference to the Best Explanation* (Lipton, 1991).[11] A notable feature of Lipton's account is that he conceives of IBE as a two-stage process, where one first *generates* a limited set of

---

[8] This definition of inference is in line with influential accounts of inference provided by Frege (1979), Boghossian (2014), and Neta (2013).

[9] In addition to those mentioned below, these include the accounts of Foster (1982), Musgrave (1988), Lycan (1988, 2012), and Weintraub (2013).

[10] See also Harman 1989, ch. 3, and Harman 1997.

[11] In chapter 7 of the second edition of his book, Lipton (2004, 103–120) suggests that IBE can be seen as a heuristic for Bayesian reasoning, which brings his account closer to what I am calling hybrid accounts (discussed in §2.4). In what follows I nevertheless refer to the second edition when discussing Lipton's original inferentialist account, since the relevant discussion is largely unchanged between the first and second editions.

competing explanatory hypotheses (the generation stage), and one then *infers* the best hypothesis that has been generated in this way (the inference stage). At both stages, explanatory considerations come into play, helping us first to come up with plausible competing explanations at the generation stage, and then to accept one of these competing explanations at the inference stage.

One way to think about this aspect of Lipton's account is in terms of comparisons with Peirce's notion of Abduction and Harman's IBE. As we have noted, Peirce's Abduction was arguably focused on the generation of theories, so Lipton's first stage of IBE may be roughly identified with Peirce's Abduction. By contrast, Harman was silent on how "alternative hypotheses" are generated; indeed, Harman did not explicitly acknowledge that there was any epistemic issue to be addressed regarding how such hypotheses would be generated. Instead, Harman's discussion of IBE is exclusively concerned with the process of inferring some hypothesis, by comparing it in terms of explanatory considerations with other hypotheses, regardless of how these other hypotheses came into consideration. To be fair, it should not be surprising that Harman, writing in 1965, would have overlooked the issue of how explanatory hypotheses are generated, since philosophers of science did not at that time generally consider such topics to be within the purview of their field (Schickore, 2022, §5).

Another distinctive feature of Lipton's account concerns what makes an explanatory hypothesis "best," or "better" than an alternative. On Lipton's account, "the best explanation [is] the one which would, if correct, be the most explanatory or provide the most understanding: the 'loveliest' explanation" (2004, 59). Lipton (2004, 61) goes on to describe his version of IBE as "Inference to the Loveliest Explanation," where "loveliness" is determined by how much understanding an explanatory hypothesis would provide if it were true. Elliott (2021) points out that in this respect Lipton's account departs from the more standard idea that explanatory goodness is determined by a list of explanatory virtues (how simple it is, how much it explains, etc.), as Harman suggests and many other proponents of IBE have maintained. In Section 3, we will examine which of these two conceptions of explanatory goodness is more plausible or congenial to accounts of abductive reasoning.

An important issue on which different inferential accounts diverge is how to conceive of the *structure* of the evaluation that takes place within abductive reasoning. As the term "Inference to the *Best* Explanation" indicates, the standard view – once again inherited from Harman (1965) – is that this is a *comparative* evaluation of one explanatory hypothesis as *better* than the set of alternative hypotheses that have been generated. Thus, on the standard conception of explanatory goodness as determined by explanatory virtues, one compares the extent to which one hypothesis exhibits various explanatory virtues to the extent to which alternative hypotheses exhibit these virtues. By contrast, there is nothing in Harman's formulation to suggest that abductive reasoning involves evaluating, in an absolute sense, whether a given hypothesis is simple *tout court*, or whether it has some specific degree of simplicity; and likewise for other explanatory virtues.[12]

This gives rise to a classic objection to IBE, pressed most influentially by Bas van Fraassen (1989).[13] Van Fraassen pointed out that, in the type of comparative evaluation that is involved in IBE, a given theory can only be reasonably judged to be better than other theories that have actually been generated, not also to be better than other theories that no one has (yet) proposed. So the "best" of these theories might very well be "the best of a bad lot" (van Fraassen, 1989, 143). The problem here is not that IBE cannot deliver a reasonable comparative evaluation of which theory, in some set of alternatives, is the most plausible or inferable. Rather, van Fraassen is pointing out that since the hypotheses one has so far generated may all be false, the true explanation might be provided by a hypothesis outside of the set of available hypotheses. In that case, IBE would lead us to a false conclusion, no matter how good we are at locating the best explanatory hypothesis among the available competitors. This is known as the *bad lot objection* and it has shaped much of the debate about IBE in the last few decades. It will be discussed at length in Section 4, along with other similar objections to IBE.

For the time being, suffice it to say that the bad lot objection has been influential in shaping contemporary accounts of abductive reasoning. In particular, the objection has motivated a number of authors – including van Fraassen himself – to formulate *non-inferential* accounts of abductive reasoning: "Despite its name, [Inference to the Best Explanation] is not the rule to infer the truth of the best available explanation. That is only a code for the real rule, which is to allocate our personal probabilities with due respect to explanation" (van Fraassen, 1989, 143). What van Fraassen is suggesting here is that abductive reasoning cannot be plausibly analyzed as a form of inference at all; instead, it may be more promising to subsume abductive reasoning under a framework for scientific reasoning in which we merely assign "personal probabilities" to theories.[14] Van Fraassen ultimately concludes that this is a dead-end as well,

---

[12] Indeed, it is not clear how to even make sense of absolute evaluations of explanatory virtues, since there doesn't seem to be a universal measure of such virtues that would apply to all or even most theories (Dellsén, 2021, 162–163).

[13] See also Sklar (1981), Stanford (2006), and Roush (2005), among others, for closely related concerns about scientific reasoning based on the fact that scientists typically have only generated a fraction of all possible theories in some domain.

[14] Despite describing "Inference to the Best Explanation" as "only code for the real rule," van Fraassen goes on to refer to the "real rule" as "Inference to the Best Explanation" as well (see

and so that we should do away with abductive reasoning entirely. However, as we shall now see, others have been inspired by van Fraassen's suggestion to develop various probability-based accounts of abductive reasoning.

2.3 Probabilistic Accounts

The hallmark of *probabilistic accounts* of abductive reasoning, as I shall be using the term, is that they attempt to capture abductive reasoning entirely within the Bayesian approach to scientific reasoning – henceforth simply *Bayesianism*. For our purposes, Bayesianism can be said to consist of the following three claims. First, scientists (and other agents) have, or can be represented as having, extremely fine-grained opinions about various states of the world. In particular, according to Bayesianism, scientists will not merely have an opinion that some hypothesis H is true or plausible; rather they will assign – or will be representable as assigning – a specific real value between 0 and 1 to H, where an assignment of 0 amounts to being certain that H is false while an assignment of 1 amounts to being certain that H is true. These fine-grained opinions are often referred to as *credences* (alternatively: *degrees of belief, degrees of confidence*), partly in order to distinguish them from more coarse-grained opinions such as (outright) acceptance and (full) belief.

Second, Bayesianism claims that in order for the agents in question to be perfectly rational, their credences must satisfy the axioms of the probability calculus. Put differently, credences must be probabilities, in the mathematical sense of the term which is defined by the probability axioms. This means, among other things, that these (rational) agents' opinions can be represented as a probability function, $Pr(\cdot)$, from any proposition to a real value between 0 and 1 (inclusive). This is the sense in which, as authors such as van Fraassen put it, a rational agent has "personal probabilities": They have credences which, if perfectly rational according to Bayesianism, count as probabilities by the mathematical definition thereof. In later years, it has become common to refer to this part of the Bayesian approach as *Probabilism*, since it demands of rational agents that their opinions be probabilities.[15]

---

also, e.g., Weisberg, 2009; Henderson, 2014; Pettigrew, 2021). By contrast, I use "Inference to the Best Explanation" to refer more narrowly to the inferential account of abductive reasoning developed by Harman and Lipton, among others.

[15] Note that Probabilism is a *normative* requirement. It says something about what combinations of credences agents *ought to* have in order to be epistemically rational, rather than what combinations of opinions they *actually have*. For example, if A entails B but not vice versa, Probabilism implies that rational agents must assign a lower credence to A than to B, since it follows from the probability axioms that the probability of A is lower than that of B.

A third and final claim made by Bayesianism concerns how perfectly rational agents should change their credences (i.e., their personal probabilities) over time, as they gain more information about the world. Put differently, it concerns how they should "update" these personal probabilities in light of new evidence. The canonical version of this claim has become known as *Bayesian Conditionalization*. It says that rational agents should update the value of their personal probability regarding some hypothesis H as they obtain some evidence E (and no other evidence) by replacing it with the value of the probability they previously assigned to H *conditional* on E, that is, the so-called *conditional probability* of H *given* E, $Pr(H|E)$. A bit more precisely:

Bayesian Conditionalization: A rational agent who obtains evidence E (and no other evidence) should set

$$Pr'(H) = Pr(H|E)$$

where $Pr(\cdot)$ and $Pr'(\cdot)$ are the agent's probability functions before and after obtaining E, respectively.[16]

Although there are other, arguably somewhat more sophisticated, versions of this Bayesian updating rule, these will – with one exception discussed immediately below – generally not be important for our purposes here, for they refine Bayesian Conditionalization in ways that do not concern abductive reasoning specifically.

Now, although the above three claims form the core of Bayesianism, the statement that is most often associated with the Bayesian approach – and from which it gets its name – is simply a mathematical theorem of the probability axioms that has proved to be extremely useful within the Bayesian approach, namely *Bayes's Theorem*:

$$Pr(H|E) = \frac{Pr(E|H)\,Pr(H)}{Pr(E)}$$

One of the reasons this simple theorem is so useful for Bayesians is that it allows them to calculate the value that one should assign to $Pr'(H)$ according to Bayesian Conditionalization: $Pr'(H) = Pr(H|E) = \frac{Pr(E|H)\,Pr(H)}{Pr(E)}$. Thus Bayesians can say something quite informative about how an agent, such as a scientist, should allocate their personal probabilities in a given case: They should take their previous probabilities, $Pr(E|H)$, $Pr(H)$, $Pr(E)$, combine these as Bayes's theorem dictates by multiplying the first two and dividing by the third, and use the resulting value as their new personal probability for H.

---

[16] $Pr(\cdot)$ and $Pr'(\cdot)$ are also referred to as the agent's *prior* and *posterior* probabilities, respectively.

With all this Bayesian machinery in our arsenal, we are now finally in a position to consider probabilistic accounts of abductive reasoning. Let us start with the approach suggested by van Fraassen (1989) following his critique of inferential accounts (see §2.2 and §4.2). (In what follows, it is worth keeping in mind that van Fraassen did not endorse the following proposal; indeed, he argued that it was irredeemably flawed, along with other attempts to spell out cogent accounts of abductive reasoning.) Van Fraassen's core idea was that in order for abductive reasoning to have a place within Bayesianism, the hypothesis that best explains some evidence E must somehow be awarded greater personal probability than Bayesian Conditionalization alone dictates. Thus, Bayesian Conditionalization must effectively be modified so that a "bonus" is added to the agent's posterior probability for a hypothesis that provides the best explanation of the relevant evidence. The simplest way to do this would be to require that agents set $Pr'(H) = Pr(H|E) + b$, where b is the probability bonus awarded to H for providing the best explanation of E. We might call this general idea *Abductive Conditionalization.*[17]

Is Abductive Conditionalization plausible? Van Fraassen argues that it is not. In short, van Fraassen's argument is that since Abductive Conditionalization requires agents to update their personal probabilities in a way that conflicts with Bayesian Conditionalization, any argument for Bayesian Conditionalization is an argument against Abductive Conditionalization. We will consider this argument in much more detail in Section 4. For now, suffice it to say that most authors – with the notable exception of Igor Douven (2013, 2022) – have agreed with van Fraassen that Abductive Conditionalization is untenable. However, few of them have concluded from this that there is no place for abductive reasoning within the Bayesian approach. Instead, they have generally rejected van Fraassen's construal of abductive reasoning in terms of bonus probabilities, and argued that the Bayesian approach can be combined with a form of abductive reasoning in a way that allows one to hold on to Bayesian Conditionalization. In this section, I will consider two specific accounts of this kind, which hold that explanatory preferences *constrain* Bayesian reasoning, on the one hand, or *emerge* from it naturally, on the other hand. (In the next section, we turn to accounts on which abductive reasoning functions as a heuristic for Bayesian reasoning, and thus allow one to hold on to Bayesian Conditionalization in a different way.)

---

[17] If H is awarded a bonus in this way, then at least some competing hypotheses must receive a penalty so as to balance the total probability awarded to H and its mutually exclusive and jointly exhaustive rivals, because the sum of these probabilities has to be 1. In principle this can be done in any number of ways, but – as we shall see below (§4.2) – Douven (2022, 51) provides a nicely conservative and mathematically satisfying way of doing this.

Perhaps the most straightforward way of finding a place for abductive reasoning within the Bayesian approach is to suggest that explanatory considerations, such as the simplicity or explanatory power of a given hypothesis relative to the evidence, determine how one should assign probabilities *before* one updates on the evidence (e.g., Huemer, 2009; Weisberg, 2009; Poston, 2014; Bird, 2017). In particular, explanatory considerations may be taken to constrain assignments of prior probabilities conditional on some evidence before one obtains that evidence. Thus, if H_2 is explanatorily better than H_1 with respect to E, this view implies that one should assign a higher value to $Pr(H_2|E)$ than to $Pr(H_1|E)$. By good old Bayesian Conditionalization, this implies that the probability one ends up assigning to H_2, that is, the posterior probability $Pr'(H_2)$, is also higher than the probability one ends up assigning to H_1, $Pr'(H_1)$. Let us call accounts of this kind *constraining probabilistic accounts* of abductive reasoning.

It may be worth delving a little deeper into how assigning a higher prior conditional probability to the better explaining H_2 than to the worse explaining H_1 would play out. Someone who starts out assigning a higher probability to H_2 given E than to H_1 given E, $Pr(H_1|E) < Pr(H_2|E)$, must by Bayes's Theorem also assign probabilities that satisfy the following inequality:[18]

$$Pr(E|H_1)\,Pr(H_1) < Pr(E|H_2)\,Pr(H_2)$$

In light of this, constraining probabilists might argue that we can identify separate constraints for the first and second terms on each side, that is, the so-called "likelihoods" $Pr(E|H_1)$ and $Pr(E|H_2)$, on the one hand, and the so-called "priors" $Pr(H_1)$ and $Pr(H_2)$, on the other. For example, purely theoretical virtues like simplicity might be taken to constrain the priors, $Pr(H_1)$ and $Pr(H_2)$; while other virtues that are more concerned with the relationship between the hypotheses and the evidence, such as explanatory power, might be taken to constrain the likelihoods $Pr(E|H_1)$ and $Pr(E|H_2)$.

Clearly, requiring that one already assigns higher prior probabilities to more explanatory hypotheses in this way ensures that there is no conflict between constraining probabilistic accounts and Bayesian Conditionalization. On the contrary, this approach *supplements* Bayesianism by providing criteria for which prior probabilities agents should start out with. Moreover, constraining probabilistic accounts are quite flexible, in that they can accommodate any judgment one might like to make regarding whether hypotheses exhibiting any particular explanatory virtue to some extent should be preferred to hypotheses

---

[18] This follows by applying Bayes's Theorem to both sides of the inequality and cancelling out $Pr(E)$, which otherwise occurs in the denominator on both sides.

that don't (or do so to a lesser extent). After all, such preferences can simply be formulated as additional constraints on the prior probabilities one should have before updating via Bayesian Conditionalization. Indeed, the preferences in question need not be explanatory in any meaningful sense, since they could literally concern any feature of the hypotheses in question whatsoever.

However, this flexibility of constraining probabilistic accounts also points to a significant weakness. The weakness is that these accounts seem particularly ill-placed to provide us with any sort of *justification* for abductive reasoning thus understood. In particular, we can ask the constraining probabilist where these constraints on rational probability assignments are supposed to come from: In virtue of what is it rational to assign a higher prior conditional probability to hypotheses that provide "better" explanations? Some constraining probabilists have suggested that only by constraining probabilities in this way can we avoid inductive skepticism, that is, the conclusion that past observations give us no justification for our predictions of future observations.[19] But it's not clear that this gives us any reason to think that rationality requires such constraints, as opposed to giving us reasons to think – wishfully – that it would be nice if it did.

In this regard, another sort of probabilistic account seems to do better. Following Henderson (2014), I will refer to these as *emergent probabilistic accounts*. Emergent probabilistic accounts do not impose any explanation-based constraints on the prior probabilities one starts out with before conditionalizing on evidence. Rather, they hold that preferences for hypotheses that provide better explanations are automatically reflected in the likelihoods of theories, given certain natural and independently-motivated assumptions about how prior probabilities should be distributed. For instance, Henderson (2014, 2017) argues that the scientific theories that provide better explanations are those whose parameters or auxiliaries require less "fine-tuning" in order for the theories to provide explanations of the relevant data. Given natural choices of prior probabilities, argues Henderson, this implies that theories which provide better explanations in this sense are also more probable according to Bayesianism. In a similar vein, McGrew (2003) argues that a theory's capacity to explain many different types of facts can be shown to pick out theories that Bayesians should regard as more probable under natural assumptions about what rational agents' prior probability distributions will be like.

---

[19] See Weisberg (2009) and especially Huemer (2009); although see also Smithson (2017) for a rebuttal of Huemer's argument.

An interestingly different emergent probabilistic account is provided by Lange (2022). Lange suggests that the preference for hypotheses that provide better explanations of some evidence E is due to the explanations being of the same kind as various explanations of other facts $E_1, \ldots, E_m$, where we have independent reasons to regard the latter explanations as correct. Provided that we have reason to be confident that the explanations of E, on the one hand, and of $E_1, \ldots, E_m$, on the other hand, will be of the same kind, Lange argues that we must, by Bayesian lights, regard the explanation of E to be more probable than it would otherwise be in virtue of its having the same kind of explanation as do $E_1, \ldots, E_m$ (Lange, 2022, 99). To illustrate with an everyday example, suppose that when an electronic device stops working in my home, it has usually or always turned out to be because a single component of that device is malfunctioning. Thus, when my remote control stops working today, I have some reason to think there is some single component of the remote that is malfunctioning – assuming of course that I regard it likely that this new event has the same type of explanation as the previous events, perhaps because all of these cases involve electronic devices. In this way, a local probabilistic preference for simpler theories would arise naturally on Lange's account, that is, without the account having to appeal to some specific list of explanatory virtues that always count in a theory's favor.

An important advantage of emergent over constraining probabilistic accounts is that the former seem to offer an independent justification for preferring more explanatory hypothesis. Rather than simply stipulating that rationality requires us to prefer more explanatory hypotheses, emergent probabilistic accounts purport to *explain* why such a preference would arise under natural assumptions about prior probability distributions. To be sure, there remains for the emergent probabilist a closely related problem of explaining why the "natural" assumptions about prior probability distributions should be taken to be correct – or indeed why they deserve to be called "natural."[20] So proponents of constraining probabilistic accounts may retort that the supposedly problematic step of postulating certain constraints on prior probabilities in order to accommodate preferences for more explanatory hypotheses has a close analogue in the arguments given by emergent probabilists.

2.4 Hybrid Accounts

Thus far we have explored inferential and probabilistic accounts of abductive reasoning, which respectively see abductive reasoning as a *sui generis*

---

[20] Here, we are bumping up against a well-known fundamental challenge for Bayesianism, namely the problem of priors (see, e.g., Easwaran, 2011, 326–327).

type of inference in which theories are accepted on the basis of explanatory considerations, on the one hand, or as a preference for better explaining theories in probabilistic updating, on the other. The third type of account combines aspects of these two types of accounts. These *hybrid accounts* hold that abductive reasoning manifests itself both as a specific type of inference, such as IBE, and also as a preference for better explaining theories in an otherwise probabilistic approach to scientific reasoning.[21]

One way to develop a hybrid account is to argue that agents engage in two quite distinct forms of abductive reasoning that have little to do with each other. In particular, one might take inspiration from epistemologists who maintain that full beliefs and credences are distinct, and yet equally real and fundamental, types of attitudes (see, e.g., Weisberg, 2020; Jackson and Tan, 2022). These two types of attitudes would give rise to two distinct forms of reasoning, inferential and probabilistic, which would occur simultaneously and independently in a single agent. Importantly for our purposes, these two forms of reasoning could both be influenced by explanatory considerations – although not necessarily the same explanatory considerations in each case. For example, one could argue that rational agents form full beliefs by employing a Harman-style IBE while simultaneously updating their personal probabilities by awarding bonuses to more explanatory theories, as per Abductive Conditionalization. We might call this a *dualistic account* of abductive reasoning.

Another way to develop a hybrid account is to argue that one of the two types of reasoning is in some way more fundamental than the other. In particular, several philosophers have suggested that some form of explanation-based inference, such as IBE, might serve as a reliable heuristic device to approximate correct probabilistic reasoning.[22] The motivating thought here is that it is generally much easier and straightforward for nonideal agents to successfully make abductive inferences such as IBE than to correctly perform any kind of probabilistic updating. After all, the latter requires agents to keep track of the probabilities they should assign at a given time to both hypotheses and potential

---

[21] To be clear, hybrid accounts need not be thought of as alternatives to inferential and probabilistic accounts; rather, it may be more fruitful to view a given hybrid account as a combination of some particular inferential or probabilistic account with some additional claims borrowed from, or inspired by, the other type of account. In particular, the specific hybrid account discussed towards the end of this section may be viewed as a combination of a probabilistic account of abductive reasoning and the claim that a form of IBE serves as a reliable heuristic for approximating the type of reasoning prescribed by that probabilistic account.

[22] Such accounts have been proposed and developed in a number of different ways in recent years, for example, by Niiniluoto (1999), Okasha (2000), Lipton (2001), McGrew (2003), Cabrera (2017), and Dellsén (2018). It has also been argued that abductive reasoning is more fundamental than Bayesian, for example, because the latter is merely an idealized model of the former (McCain and Moretti, 2022).

evidence, which in turn requires repeatedly calculating conditional probabilities from priors and likelihoods. By contrast, an inferential procedure such as IBE does not require agents to assign probabilities to anything, or to constantly update those probabilities in light of new information. All it requires is that agents occasionally estimate how well a number of already-formulated theories explain the evidence they have obtained at that time.

The thought that probabilistic reasoning is too difficult for ordinary agents is supported by robust psychological results suggesting that people are in general prone to systematic biases in probabilistic reasoning, and that such biases are present even among those who are familiar with probabilistic reasoning (see, e.g., Kahneman et al., 1982; Kahneman, 2011). These results indicate that it may be a bad idea for ordinary agents to even try to engage directly in probabilistic reasoning on a day-to-day basis – even if such probabilistic updating is what is ideally rational (i.e., rational for ideal agents that don't suffer from systematic biases and other cognitive limitations). Furthermore, whether or not we *ought* to engage in probabilistic updating, it seems quite clear from these results that few of us *do* engage in it, except perhaps when we are specifically prompted to do so, for example, when the hypotheses in question explicitly refer to probabilities. In Kahneman's terminology, we mostly engage in the faster and more automatic "System 1" thinking, as opposed to the slower and more effortful "System 2" thinking in which careful probabilistic calculations would take place.

These considerations give rise to what we may call the *heuristic account* of abductive reasoning. On this account, the ideal form of scientific reasoning would be probabilistic through and through. However, since ordinary agents are often unable or poorly situated to engage in such reasoning, they approximate it by instead making abductive inferences, such as IBEs, which deliver results sufficiently similar to those that would result from reasoning probabilistically in an ideally rational way. In contrast to the dualistic account sketched above, the heuristic account thus sees probabilistic reasoning as normatively more fundamental, in that it is the ultimate standard of evaluation for scientific reasoning that abductive inferences should in some way approximate. With that said, proponents of heuristic accounts typically argue that abductive inferences are more ubiquitous than explicitly probabilistic reasoning, in that it is the type of reasoning in which most human agents in fact most commonly engage (see, e.g., Keil, 2006; Lombrozo, 2010).

Of course, abductive inference can only serve as a heuristic in this way if it does in fact approximate normatively correct probabilistic reasoning. With that said, abductive inference need not accord with probabilistic reasoning exactly and in every case in order to serve as a heuristic in this sense, since — just as with any other heuristic — it may fail in extraordinary cases and provide only a rough guide in normal cases. So does abductive inference at least approximate normatively correct probabilistic reasoning in most, or at least many, cases? In order to make the case that it does, the heuristic account may take a leaf out of the book of probabilistic accounts, which (let us recall) suggest that preferences for better explaining hypotheses either constrain, or emerge from, rational agents' prior probability assignments. In either case, it seems that we should expect abductive inferences generally to recommend accepting the theories that are most probable by Bayesian lights, because both forms of reasoning are influenced by the same set of considerations, namely explanatory considerations.

To illustrate this point, consider Okasha's (2000) example of a doctor who examines an injured child and forms two competing hypotheses: that they have pulled a muscle (H_1); and that they have torn a ligament (H_2). The doctor decides that H_2 offers the better explanation of the observed symptoms and, using IBE, therefore tentatively accepts H_2. When asked to explain her reasoning, the doctor says: "firstly, preadolescent children very rarely pull muscles, but often tear ligaments. Secondly, the symptoms, though compatible with either diagnosis, are exactly what we would expect if the child has torn a ligament, though not if [the child] has pulled a muscle. Therefore the second hypothesis is preferable" (Okasha, 2000, 703). According to Okasha, this reasoning coincides with the following probabilistic argument for assigning a higher probability to H_2 than to H_1: "given the background information, the prior probability of H_2 is higher than that of H_1 [i.e., $Pr(H_1) < Pr(H_2)$]; the probability of the evidence conditional on H_2 is greater than its probability conditional on H_1 [i.e., $Pr(E|H_1) < Pr(E|H_2)$], therefore the posterior probability of H_2 is greater than that of H_1 [i.e., $Pr'(H_1) < Pr'(H_2)$]" (Okasha, 2000, 702–703).[23]

Note, though, that Okasha's suggestion about IBE coinciding with probabilistic updating only works if we go along with his probabilistic assumptions, that is, that $Pr(H_1) < Pr(H_2)$ and $Pr(E|H_1) < Pr(E|H_2)$. This is of course precisely what probabilistic accounts suggest we should do in different ways. Specifically, constraining probabilistic accounts hold that because H_2 explains better than H_1, rationality requires us to assign probabilities so as to favor H_2 over H_1 in some such way; while emergent probabilistic accounts hold that this probabilistic favoring of H_2 over H_1 falls out of other, independently-motivated constraints on prior probability assignments. By contrast, if one completely rejects the idea that more explanatory hypotheses should be assigned higher

---

[23] To see why the third inequality follows from the first two, recall from Section 2.3 that $Pr'(H_1) < Pr'(H_2)$ is, given Bayesian Conditionalization, equivalent to $Pr(E|H_1) Pr(H_1) < Pr(E|H_2) Pr(H_2)$.

prior probabilities, then Okasha's suggestion will not be compelling, for then the doctor's IBE-based inference might coincide with it being rational to assign lower probabilities to hypotheses that provide "better" explanations, for example, in that $Pr(H_1) > Pr(H_2)$ and/or $Pr(H_1|E) > Pr(H_2|E)$ (Weisberg, 2009, 132–136). For this reason, heuristic accounts of abductive reasoning must arguably assume that rational probability assignments favor hypotheses that provide better explanations, as per probabilistic accounts.

Another issue for heuristic accounts concerns what sort of conclusion an abductive inference would warrant while at the same time approximating probabilistic reasoning. Initially one might have hoped that abductive inferences would warrant something like a high probability assignment to (and thus, perhaps, a full belief in)[24] the inferred hypothesis. However, note that this is not the type of conclusion that is drawn in Okasha's example, where the doctor merely concludes that "the posterior probability of H_2 is greater than that of H_1," that is, that $Pr'(H_1) < Pr'(H_2)$. This is a comparative claim, regarding the relative probabilities of H_1 and H_2. As such it is compatible with H_1 and H_2 being assigned arbitrarily low probabilities in absolute terms, and so would not necessarily warrant an assignment of high probability to (let alone full belief in) either H_1 or H_2. Indeed, it is hard to see how the doctor's abductive reasoning in Okasha's example could provide her with a conclusion more definite than the claim about the relative probabilities of H_1 and H_2, since even the abductive argument deals in comparative claims about which type of injury is *more common* in children, on the one hand, and which injury *better fits* the symptoms, on the other.

One might think that this comparative structure to Okasha's example is incidental, and that a heuristic account could be developed in which abductive inference serves as a heuristic for absolute, as opposed to merely comparative, probability assignments. However, Dellsén (2018, 1753–1760) presents a problem for heuristic accounts of this sort. As should be apparent from how Bayes's Theorem combines with Bayesian Conditionalization (see §2.3), the absolute posterior probability of H_1, $Pr'(H_1)$, is determined not only by the prior $Pr(H_1)$ and the likelihood $Pr(E|H_1)$, but also by $Pr(E)$. This term – the probability of the evidence itself, sometimes called the *marginal likelihood* – is notoriously difficult to estimate with any reliability, because Bayesianism dictates that it must be equal to a weighted sum of the priors and likelihoods of all competing hypotheses in logical space, including not only H_1 and H_2 but also any other hypotheses that are yet to be formulated – and perhaps never

---

[24] The parenthetical remark assumes a "Lockean" account of the relationship between personal probability and full belief (see, e.g., Foley, 1992).

will (see, e.g., Shimony, 1970; Salmon, 1990; Roush, 2005).[25] Moreover, the various explanatory considerations that are supposed to guide abductive inference do not seem to be of much help in estimating this term, since they refer to either to features of the hypotheses themselves or their relationship with the evidence, not to features of *other* hypotheses or *their* relationship with the evidence.

For these sorts of reasons, Dellsén (2018) suggests that IBE cannot generally serve as a reliable heuristic for absolute probability assignments. However, on Dellsén's view, this does not spell disaster for the heuristic account of abductive reasoning, since IBE can still serve as a reliable heuristic for probabilistic comparisons of the sort we saw in Okasha's example. Although such comparative conclusions are sometimes less informative than we would like – since they don't tell us how confident we ought to be that a specific theory is true – they can still provide a great deal of rational guidance for the practicing scientist. For example, the comparative conclusion that H_2 (torn ligament) is more probable than H_1 (pulled muscle) might prompt Okasha's doctor to order diagnostic tests focused on the child's ligament rather than the muscle. In this sense, H_2 becomes the doctor's "working hypothesis." So, in short, the comparative conclusion that some particular hypotheses are more probable than their rivals can help practicing scientists to focus their subsequent investigations on the most probable of such hypotheses.

It's worth noting that Dellsén's argument that IBE can only serve as a heuristic for probabilistic comparisons is targeted at standard formulations of IBE of the sort advocated by Harman (1965) and Lipton (2004). Thus an alternative way to avoid the argument is to modify one's account of IBE, or abductive inference more generally, so that it better fits with what is required of rational agents who wish to make absolute probability assignments. A plausible thought is that this might be done by requiring not only that the inferred hypothesis provides a *better* explanation than its extant rivals, but also that the explanation be *good enough* in some sense (Musgrave, 1988; Lipton, 2004). Indeed, Dellsén (2021) makes a concrete suggestion along these lines, arguing that a more demanding form of IBE – which requires an agent to go through a temporally extended process of gathering more evidence and attempting to formulate superior explanations – is capable of delivering absolute verdicts. We will examine this suggestion, along with other similar suggestions, in Section 4. For now, however, let us simply note that such suggestions involve modifying IBE quite substantially from what it is normally taken to involve.

---

[25] That is, $Pr(E) = \sum_{k=1}^{n} Pr(H_k) Pr(E|H_k)$, where $H_1, \ldots, H_n$ are mutually exclusive and jointly exhaustive hypotheses.

3 Why Prefer Explanatory Hypotheses?

This section focuses on the fact that in abductive reasoning, one infers or assigns a higher probability to the hypothesis that *best explains* one's evidence. But what grounds, if any, are there for preferring hypotheses that provide better explanations in this way? To begin to answer this question, we'll start by considering in more detail what different authors mean by saying that one hypothesis provides a "better explanation" than another (§3.1). We then contrast two quite different possible reasons for preferring better explanations, based respectively on epistemic and pragmatic considerations (§3.2). These contrasting views are then put to the test in the following two sections by considering two different ways in which some hypotheses are often said to explain better than others, namely, with respect to the extent to which the hypothesis explains a greater range of phenomena (§3.3), and the extent to which the hypothesis posits fewer things with which to do the explaining (§3.4).

3.1 Conceptions of Explanatory Goodness

In order to address the question of what justifies a preference for hypotheses that best explain one's evidence, we must first get clearer on what might be meant by saying that one hypothesis "explains better" than another hypothesis. In short, we must ask: What is explanatory goodness?

The most popular answer to this question derives from Harman (1965). Recall that according to Harman, the judgment that one hypothesis explains better than another "will [presumably] be based on considerations such as which hypothesis is simpler, which is more plausible, which explains more, which is less *ad hoc*, and so forth" (Harman, 1965, 89). Harman's suggestion, then, is to conceive of explanatory goodness in terms of a list of seemingly independent factors, now often referred to as *explanatory virtues*, which jointly determine the explanatory goodness of a given hypothesis. This idea has been adopted by most theorists of abductive reasoning, many of whom have also developed it by providing their own list of such virtues, and associated descriptions of what they amount to (e.g., Thagard, 1978; Lycan, 1985; Mackonis, 2011; Poston, 2014). Call this *the virtue-theoretic conception* of explanatory goodness.

A crucial question for the virtue-theoretic conception is, of course, which factors count as "explanatory virtues" for its purposes. Among the more popular and widely discussed such virtues are the following:[26]

---

[26] See Beebe (2009) for an unusually comprehensive list of various proposed explanatory virtues.

Scope: How many different phenomena (or types thereof) would the hypothesis explain?

Parsimony: How few new entities (or types thereof) are posited by the hypothesis or its explanations?

Unification: To what extent does the hypothesis unify otherwise disparate phenomena (or types thereof)?

Plausibility: How well does the hypothesis fit what one already takes oneself to know?

Analogy: How similar is the hypothesis' explanations to other established explanations?

Numerous other putative explanatory virtues have been proposed as well, such as: the simplicity or elegance with which the hypothesis is formulated; its fertility or fruitfulness for further research; the testability or falsifiability of the hypothesis; and the extent to which it doesn't contain ad hoc elements. Moreover, various authors use different terms for the virtues described above.[27] It should be said that many of the features that have been described as explanatory virtues in the context of abductive reasoning have long been thought of as good-making features of scientific theories even by authors who might not consider themselves proponents of abductive reasoning (e.g., Kuhn, 1977; Quine and Ullian, 1978; Laudan, 1984).[28]

There is considerable disagreement regarding which of these features should be taken to be operative in abductive reasoning. Consider, for example, the supposed explanatory virtue of testability, which refers to the extent to which a theory has readily testable consequences (see, e.g., Lycan, 1988, 138; Beebe, 2009, 611). Although it would of course be good, in a general sense of the term, to have theories that are more testable, it does not seem plausible that the testability of a theory makes it more likely to be true. Rather, testability is a good-making feature only in that it will be *easier to find out* whether more testable theories are true. Similarly, whether or not a theory is formulated in a conceptually simple or elegant way is arguably not something that indicates that the theory is more likely to be true[29]; rather, it merely suggests that the theory

---

[27] For example, it is quite common to use "simplicity" for what I call "parsimony." This can be misleading because, as noted above, there is another kind of simplicity which concerns the way in which a theory is formulated. "Parsimony," by contrast, refers to the ontological commitments made by the theory rather than any aspect of how it is formulated.

[28] Indeed, Elliott (2021) suggests that there is nothing specifically *explanatory* about at least some of these features, and that they should therefore be described as "theoretical" rather than "explanatory" virtues.

[29] For a quick argument to that effect, note that a simply or elegantly stated theory will be materially equivalent to any number of more cumbersomely stated theories. Since materially

is easier to work with, for example because it's easier to derive predictions and explanations from it.

To analyze this situation, it can be helpful to bring in a distinction between *epistemic* and *pragmatic* virtues. Epistemic virtues are features of a theory that provide some indication, however fallible, that the virtuous theory is more likely to be true. Pragmatic virtues, by contrast, are features that come with some pragmatic or practical benefit, such as making it more convenient to use the theory for various purposes. In principle, a given explanatory virtue could be both epistemic and pragmatic, but oftentimes calling something a pragmatic virtue tacitly carries the implication that it is not also an epistemic virtue. For instance, in light of the previous paragraph, it seems plausible that testability and simplicity/elegance are (merely) pragmatic virtues. By contrast, most proponents of abductive reasoning argue that at least some of the other virtues listed above, for example, scope and parsimony, are epistemic virtues, although they don't always agree on which ones enjoy this special status. (More on these virtues in §§3.3–3.4 below.).

Regardless of which explanatory virtues are operative in abductive reasoning, and whether these are epistemic or (merely) pragmatic, one might wonder how exactly these virtues are supposed to determine the overall explanatory goodness of a hypothesis. This issue has been addressed in some detail regarding theory choice in general, where Okasha (2011) in effect argues that certain seemingly-plausible constraints on determining which theory does best overall with respect to some number of explanatory virtues cannot all be satisfied. In particular, Okasha suggests that – contrary to what one might have thought beforehand – determining which theory does best overall requires one to estimate not only which theories do better than other theories with regard to particular virtues, but also *how much better* these theories are doing with regard to these virtues. If Okasha is right, then a scientist who wants to determine which theory provides the overall best explanation must find some way of measuring how much more or less scope, parsimony, and so forth, each theory has in comparison to its rivals.[30]

Thus far we have considered the virtue-theoretic conception of explanatory goodness in various guises. The virtue-theoretic conception is assumed in most discussions of abductive reasoning, but Lipton (2004), interestingly, appears to

---

equivalent theories are, necessarily, equally likely to be true, it follows that a theory's simplicity (in this sense of the term – see footnote 27) cannot be positively correlated with its probability.

[30] For a critical discussion of Okasha's argument, see Morreau (2015) and Stegenga (2015); although see also Okasha (2015) for replies. In a somewhat different context, Priest (2016) provides a nicely precise way of aggregating theoretical virtues that would be congenial to Okasha's suggestion.

endorse an alternative conception of explanatory goodness. On Lipton's view, explanatory goodness (or "loveliness," as he calls it) is determined by how much understanding an explanatory hypothesis would provide if it were true. The greater or deeper the understanding that would be provided by the hypothesis, the "lovelier" it is – and to that extent it is to be preferred or inferred in IBE (Lipton, 2004, 59–60). Following Elliott (2021), let us call this *the subjunctive conception* of explanatory goodness.

Now, the subjunctive and virtue-theoretic conceptions of explanatory goodness are clearly conceptually distinct, so one might suspect that Lipton's endorsement of the subjunctive conception would be backed up by arguments against the virtue-theoretic conception. Not so. Instead, Lipton (2004, 122–123) adopts a conciliatory position according to which our judgments of the relative "loveliness" of two explanatory hypotheses (made according to the subjunctive conception) tend to match the extent to which the explanatory virtues favor one of the hypotheses over the other. It should be said, however, that Lipton's discussion of this issue is brief, and Lipton is explicitly noncommittal about what counts as an explanatory virtue. Furthermore, Lipton says little about what it is for one hypothesis to provide us with "more understanding" than another, that is, what "loveliness" consists in. This makes Lipton's proposal difficult to evaluate.

A more thorough examination of the issue is provided by Elliott (2021), who argues that the subjunctive and virtue-theoretic conceptions often diverge in their judgments regarding whether one hypothesis explains "better" than another (see also Barnes, 1995). For example, Elliott contrasts two hypotheses that could be used to explain why we can observe light from stars that are extremely far away. The first is the commonly accepted hypothesis that "the universe is around 13.8 billion years old and the speed of light is constant in a vacuum." This explains why we see such distant stars by assuming that light has had a very long time to travel, at a constant speed, from the stars to us. A second hypothesis, inspired by creationism, is that "the universe is 6,000-10,000 years old and the speed of light has been slowing since the creation of the universe." This hypothesis purports to explain why we can see distant stars by assuming that light was travelling at a much greater speed, allowing it to cover all that distance between us and them in only 6,000–10,000 years. Now, the first of these hypotheses seems to exhibit the theoretical virtues to a greater degree than the second, for example in that it has greater plausibility in light of background knowledge, and is less ad hoc in so far as it posits a constant where the second posits a variable that must be fine-tuned to explain the data. However, according to Elliott, neither hypothesis would, if true, provide more understanding than the other. After all, each one would, if true, make our observations of distant stars perfectly comprehensible, leaving no mystery as to why these stars are visible.

From this example and others like it Elliott concludes that the two conceptions – the subjective and the virtue-theoretic – are not extensionally equivalent. Furthermore, since the first of the above hypotheses is clearly more plausible than the second, the virtue-theoretic conception is better suited to spelling out the notion of explanatory goodness with which a plausible account of abductive reasoning would operate. Thus, not only do the subjunctive and virtue-theoretic conceptions diverge; when they do diverge, Elliott suggests that the virtue-theoretic conception should be preferred over the subjunctive alternative that Lipton seems to endorse. A further reason to prefer the virtue-theoretic conception is that it is quite unclear what the subjunctive conception amounts to, since Lipton does not say what it would be for one hypothesis to provide "more understanding" than another. At the very least, it seems clear that the subjunctive conception is at this point not yet sufficiently developed to challenge the virtue-theoretic conception. For this reason, I will for the most part assume a virtue-theoretic conception in what remains of this Element.

3.2 Do Explanatory Virtues Track Truth?

In light of the previous section, it seems that the most plausible conception of what it is for one hypothesis to "explain better" than another appeals to various explanatory virtues. Equipped with this conception of what explanatory goodness would be, let us now turn to the question of why we should prefer hypotheses that provide better explanations in this sense. (We should keep in mind, however, that one's view of why explanatorily better theories should be preferred will clearly depend, at least to some extent, on what explanatory goodness is. In particular, certain views about why explanatorily better theories should be preferred work best when the list of explanatory virtues is restricted to those that are plausibly viewed as epistemic, as opposed to merely pragmatic, virtues.)

The simplest and perhaps most popular answer is that we should prefer hypotheses that explain better because they are more likely to be true – or, perhaps, more likely to be approximately true.[31] Given the virtue-theoretic conception of explanatory goodness, this amounts to the view that the explanatory virtues that are operative in abductive reasoning are *truth-conducive*: if a hypothesis possesses these virtues to a greater extent than alternatives, that

---

[31] I will drop this qualification in what follows to simplify discussion, but see Psillos (1999) and especially Niiniluoto (2018) on the issue of approximate truth and its relation to abductive reasoning.

hypothesis is thereby more likely to be true, other things being equal. Since the idea that established scientific theories are likely to be true is often associated with *scientific realism* (Chakravartty, 2017, §1.1), let us call this view *realism about explanatory goodness*. As we shall see, there are two importantly different versions of this view. These hold, respectively, that there are empirical reasons for thinking that better explaining hypotheses are more likely to be true – call this *a posteriori realism* – and that this can be demonstrated without appealing to empirical considerations – call this *a priori realism*.

One can of course reject both types of realism about explanatory goodness. *Antirealism about explanatory goodness* holds that better explaining hypotheses are not, as such, likelier to be true than those that explain worse. Given the virtue-theoretic conception of explanatory goodness, this amounts to the view that the explanatory virtues that are operative in abductive reasoning are *not* truth-conducive. Now, antirealists generally think that at least some explanatory virtues are pragmatic virtues, so there is a sense in which they endorse abductive reasoning, albeit only for pragmatic purposes (van Fraassen, 1980, 87–90). Let us call this *pragmatic antirealism*. With that said, antirealists could also reject entirely the idea that explanatory goodness, or explanatory virtues, have any role to play in science. In that case, there would arguably be little left to endorse in the idea of abductive reasoning, so antirealists of this ilk would really be suggesting to do away with abductive reasoning entirely. Let us call this *eliminative antirealism*.

Arguments for and against various realist and antirealists views of explanatory goodness have tended to focus on the truth-conduciveness of some particular explanatory virtue or virtues. Indeed, as we shall see, it is perfectly reasonable to hold that some of the explanatory virtues with which abductive reasoning operates are truth-conducive while others are not, and so be a realist about some virtues an antirealist about others. In order to focus the discussion, let us concentrate on two of the more widely discussed explanatory virtues, namely scope and parsimony. As we shall see, the debates between realists and antirealists regarding these two virtues play out in quite different ways.

3.3 Scope: Explaining More

Let's start by considering *scope*. Recall that this refers to the extent to which a given hypothesis explains many different phenomena (or types thereof). This feature of some theories was famously discussed by William Whewell (1858), who coined the term "consilience of inductions." For Whewell, this term applies to cases in which a theory receives support from different or unrelated pieces of evidence, as opposed to being supported by evidence that is similar or closely related. Whewell argued that this amounts to an especially powerful reason to accept a theory:

> That rules springing from remote and unconnected quarters should thus leap to the same point, can only arise from that being the point where the truth resides. […] Accordingly the cases in which inductions from classes of facts altogether different have thus jumped together, belong only to the best established theories which the history of science contains (Whewell, 1858, 88).

Whewell's point here is not just that a theory is more likely to be true if it fits a greater amount of evidence, but that the theory is especially likely to be true if the various pieces of evidence that support it are "altogether different".

For a concrete example of how this explanatory virtue gets used in scientific reasoning, consider Darwin's argumentative strategy in *On the Origin of Species* (1962). Darwin went to great lengths to present various different types of facts in support of his theory. That is, Darwin did not simply appeal to a single type of evidence over and over, even though that would certainly have been much easier. Instead, Darwin appealed to, among other things: (i) differences in flora and fauna across regions separated by geographical barriers, such as oceans; (ii) similarities in certain parts of the anatomies of entirely distinct species, such as the human hand and the wings of bats; and (iii) fossil records of some now-extinct ancestors to current species. Indeed, when summarizing his case for natural selection, Darwin explicitly notes that his theory explains "several large classes of facts" (Darwin, 1962, 476), suggesting that his argument was deliberately driven by the desire to demonstrate his theory's superior scope.

How might a realist about explanatory goodness argue that scope is an indicator of truth? One possibility is to take an empirical, or a posteriori, approach. In particular, one might suggest that the history of science is full of examples in which a theory that explains a greater number of different phenomena has turned out to be true more often than rival theories that explain less. This seems to have been Whewell's approach, who examined a number of the "best established" physical theories of the day and concluded that a great many exhibited "consilience," that is, scope, to an impressive extent.[32] One problem with this approach, however, is that in order to evaluate consilience is an indicator of *truth* one would have to assume that the supposedly "best established" theories at a given time are also true (or at least approximately true). Antirealists about

---

[32] For some more recent implementation of this type of strategy of arguing for the truth-conduciveness of explanatory goodness generally, see Boyd (1980), McMullin (1987), Salmon (1990), and Psillos (1999).

explanatory goodness might legitimately complain that such an assumption is blatantly question-begging, since they generally reject that the theories that are considered "best established" at a given time are also true (or approximately true). Furthermore, the antirealist might reject such an assumption on empirical grounds of their own, by pointing out that many of the theories on which Whewell bases his argument, such as Newton's law of universal gravitation and Fresnel's wave theory of light, have now been superseded by substantially different theories of these phenomena.

Realists about scope may therefore instead take a nonempirical, a priori, approach. This would involve arguing that there is something about the very concept of scope as an explanatory virtue from which it follows that theories with greater scope are more likely to be true. It is not clear how such an argument would proceed, since it seems clear that it is epistemically possible for theories with less scope to be more frequently true. For this reason, an entirely a priori argument for the unrestricted conclusion that scope is always truth-conducive does not seem promising. One might instead settle for something more modest, such as showing that there are certain commonly-satisfied conditions under which such an a priori argument would go through. This is, in effect, what some authors (e.g., Horwich, 1982; Earman, 1992; McGrew, 2003) have done by proving or appealing to certain results in probability theory, where the probabilistic results themselves are a priori while it is a posteriori whether the conditions in which they are applicable are satisfied in a given case.

To get a sense for how these results work, consider a simple scenario in which one hypothesis, H_1, explains some fact E_1 but not another fact E_2; while another hypothesis, H_2, explains both E_1 and E_2 (and all else is equal). What needs to be shown is that after obtaining E_1 and E_2, the posterior probability of H_2 would be higher than that of H_1. Given Bayesian Conditionalization, this should occur just in case one already assigns a higher probability to H_2 conditional on $E_1 \& E_2$ than to H_1 conditional on $E_1 \& E_2$, that is, $Pr(H_1|E_1 \& E_2) < Pr(H_2|E_1 \& E_2)$. We already encountered this type of inequality in Section 2.3, except that in place of a single "E" we now have "$E_1 \& E_2$." Thus, for analogous reasons, this inequality holds just in case:

$$Pr(E_1 \& E_2|H_1)\, Pr(H_1) < Pr(E_1 \& E_2|H_2)\, Pr(H_2)$$

In order to hold all else equal, we may suppose that H_1 and H_2 do not differ in their priors, so that $Pr(H_1) = Pr(H_2)$. In that case the inequality reduces to:

$$Pr(E_1 \& E_2|H_1) < Pr(E_1 \& E_2|H_2)$$

Since we are assuming that H_2 explains both E_1 and E_2, while H_1 explains only E_1, it might already seem plausible that H_2 confers a higher likelihood on $E_1\&E_2$, that is, that the above inequality holds. However, to see more clearly why this would be, let us rewrite each side of the inequality using the probabilistic conjunction rule (which is another theorem of the probability axioms):

$$Pr(E_1|H_1)\,Pr(E_2|E_1\&H_1) < Pr(E_1|H_2)\,Pr(E_2|E_1\&H_2)$$

Since H_1 and H_2 both explain E_1, and all else is assumed to be equal, let us also assume that $Pr(E_1|H_1) = Pr(E_1|H_2)$. In that case, the above inequality simplifies to:

$$Pr(E_2|H_1\&E_1) < Pr(E_2|H_2\&E_1) \qquad\qquad (*)$$

Here, we have the key inequality to consider for comparisons of explanatory scope. If (and only if) this inequality holds do the different pieces of evidence E_1 and E_2 confer a greater probability on H_2 than on H_1.

To see why it seems plausible that such an inequality would hold, recall first that we are assuming that H_2 explains E_2 but that H_1 does not. For this reason, it seems that H_2 by itself would confer a greater likelihood on E_2 than H_1 would by itself. However, notice that the likelihoods in $(*)$ are likelihoods of E_2 on the *conjunctions* $H_1\&E_1$ and $H_2\&E_1$. It is here that the fact that E_1 and E_2 are different types of evidence comes to the fore. It is because E_1 and E_2 are of different types that the fact that only H_2 explains E_2 makes a real difference to the likelihoods of E_2 on $H_1\&E_1$ and $H_2\&E_1$ respectively. Otherwise, namely if E_1 and E_2 were the same type of evidence, the inclusion of E_1 in each conjunction would by itself raise each likelihood of E_2, so that $Pr(E_2|H_1\&E_1)$ and $Pr(E_2|H_2\&E_1)$ would both be very high, and thus plausibly close to equal.[33] By contrast, if and in so far as E_1 and E_2 are different types of evidence, it seems that $Pr(E_2|H_1\&E_1)$ would be much lower than $Pr(E_2|H_2\&E_1)$ in virtue of H_2 being the only one of the two hypotheses that explains E_2.

To illustrate this point, let us return to Darwin's evidence for natural selection. Consider that Darwin appeals to both biological differences across geographically separated regions (E_g), on the one hand, and anatomical similarities across different biological species (E_a). And let's contrast Darwin's theory of natural selection (H_n), which explains both E_g and E_a, with a theory that explains only E_g but not E_a, such as the theory that God created different species specifically to inhabit different geographical regions (H_c). Now, because

---

[33] For example, suppose E_1 is the evidence that a thousand ravens observed within some geographical region have all turned out to be black, and E_2 is the evidence that yet another raven also turned out to be black. In that case, it seems plausible that $Pr(E_2|H_1\&E_1)$ and $Pr(E_2|H_2\&E_1)$ would both be close to 1, and thus close to equal, regardless of the content of H_1 and H_2.

this alternative theory H_c fails to explain E_a, and because E_g is a quite different type of evidence than E_a – in the sense that one wouldn't expect E_a to be the case just because E_g is the case – it seems that $Pr(E_a|H_c\&E_g)$ would be quite low. At the very least, $Pr(E_a|H_c\&E_g)$ will be low compared to $Pr(E_a|H_n\&E_g)$, since H_n does explain E_a: anatomical similarities between species are, according to natural selection, explained by the fact that the species have a common ancestry from which their anatomy has evolved. Thus $Pr(E_a|H_c\&E_g) < Pr(E_a|H_n\&E_g)$. Assuming all else is equal, and by the same probabilistic derivation as earlier, we would thus have that H_n ends up with a higher posterior probability than H_c: $P'(H_c) < P'(H_n)$.

So we seem to have grounds for preferring hypotheses that explain a greater range of different types of evidence, based in part on certain (a priori) facts about probabilistic inequalities. How might an antirealist about explanatory goodness respond to this argument? The most promising line of objection would seem to involve not objecting to the probabilistic results themselves – which follow from the probability axioms and are thus beyond reasonable dispute – but rather to some of the assumptions or interpretations of these results. For instance, an antirealist might argue that the fact that H_2 explains unrelated pieces of evidence E_1 and E_2 does not imply that the inequality (∗) holds. After all, the antirealist might respond, it's not probabilistically incoherent to assign probabilities such as to violate this inequality, even in cases of unrelated evidence such as Darwin's evidence for natural selection. There is nothing intrinsically incoherent about someone who assigns probabilities in some other way, provided of course that they take care to assign probabilities to other hypotheses in accordance with the probability calculus.

If there is a sense in which the fact that E_1 and E_2 are unrelated implies that one must assign probabilities so that (∗) holds, the above argument would seem to assume that there are constraints on permissible probability assignments beyond merely satisfying the probability axioms. Perhaps it is simply part of what it is to be fully rational to assign probabilities in such a way that for unrelated pieces of evidence, one's probability assignments satisfy (∗). However, the antirealist might easily reject any such requirements as obscure or unmotivated. This is basically the line taken by van Fraassen, who argues that there are no substantive constraints on permissible probability functions beyond satisfying the probability axioms (van Fraassen, 1984, 2000). This means that while an agent is certainly epistemically permitted to assign a higher probability to $Pr(E_2|H_2\&E_1)$ than to $Pr(E_2|H_1\&E_1)$, in accordance with (∗), she is by no means epistemically obligated to do so. This fits van Fraassen's more general "voluntarist" epistemology, on which there are minimal constraints on what agents are epistemically permitted to believe (van Fraassen, 2002, 2007).

Let us take stock. One of the most celebrated of the explanatory virtues is scope, the extent to which a given hypothesis explains many different phenomena, or types thereof. Realists regarding scope hold that it is an epistemic virtue, that is, that hypotheses with greater scope are more likely to be true; whereas antirealists hold that scope is, at most, a merely pragmatic consideration. Some realists have argued their case by pointing to a supposed empirical correlation between greater scope and (approximate) truth, but these arguments are based on assumptions that antirealists have rejected as empirically false or question-begging. A more promising argument for realism regarding scope appeals to probability theory. If successful, this argument shows that hypotheses with greater scope will – all other things being equal, and under certain plausible conditions – have a greater probability of being true.

3.4 Parsimony: Positing Less

Let us move on to the other explanatory virtue on which we'll be focusing, *parsimony*. In most discussions, parsimony is defined as the extent to which a hypothesis or its explanations postulate fewer new entities, or types thereof, where "entities" is understood broadly to include anything that could be said to exist.[34] Parsimony is sometimes referred to as *ontological simplicity*, where the qualifier "ontological" – although unfortunately sometimes dropped – indicates that it is not to be confused with other forms of simplicity. In particular, a theory is sometimes said to be simpler in the sense of consisting of fewer distinct claims or principles; this is often referred to as *syntactic simplicity* or *elegance* (Baker, 2022). By contrast, parsimony (i.e., ontological simplicity) concerns not the number of claims or principles that constitute the theory itself, but the number of entities, or types thereof, to which the theory is ontologically committed. In short, parsimony concerns the simplicity of the world according to the theory, whereas syntactic simplicity or elegance concerns the simplicity of the theory in and of itself.[35]

---

[34] A distinction is sometimes drawn between *qualitative* and *quantitative* parsimony (Lewis, 1973, 87). Qualitative parsimony is the extent to which a hypothesis or its explanations posit fewer new *types* of entities. Quantitative parsimony, by contrast, is the extent to which the hypothesis or its explanations posit fewer entities, regardless of whether they are of the same type or not. It is controversial whether the latter should be counted among the explanatory virtues, and if so, whether it is truth-conducive (see Nolan, 1997; Baker, 2003; Jansson and Tallant, 2017). In order to side-step this issue, I will throughout use "parsimony" in a general sense that might refer either to qualitative or quantitative parsimony, or indeed to both.

[35] As noted in footnote 29, it is hard to see how syntactic simplicity (i.e., elegance) could be truth-conducive, since materially equivalent theories stated in different ways might differ greatly in this respect and yet necessarily be equally probable.

It is sometimes suggested that parsimony can be shown to be truth-conducive in a rather trivial way. This involves comparing two hypotheses, H_1 and H_2, where H_2 is identical to H_1 except that H_1 postulates some entities (or types thereof) not postulated by H_2. If all else is equal, then H_1 and H_2 will nevertheless explain the same range of phenomena, and more generally be equally virtuous in other respects. Thus, there is a clear sense in which the additional entities (or types thereof) posited by H_1 are explanatorily superfluous, and in that way arguably unjustified (Schindler, 2018, 31–38). In a similar vein, one might point out that if H_1 is identical to H_2 except in postulating additional entities (or types thereof), then the probability of H_2 must be higher than that of H_1 (Sober, 2015, 71). To see why, note that H_2 would be true in all possible scenarios in which H_1 is true but not *vice versa* – in particular, H_1 would not be true if its additional entities (or types thereof) fail to exist, whereas in that case H_2 might still be true.[36]

However, this type of argument provides only a very limited defense of the idea that parsimony is truth-conducive. After all, it applies only to cases in which considerations of parsimony are brought in to adjudicate between theories that are *identical* except in that one postulates additional entities (or types thereof) not posited by the other. Such cases are atypical. Much more common are cases in which each theory posits some entities (or types thereof) not posited by the other. In such cases, although there is a difference in the number of entities (or types thereof) posited by each theory, it is not the case that the theory which posits the greater number of new entities (or types thereof) posits all the entities (or types thereof) posited by the other theory. Relatedly, these cases are generally not such that some of the entities (or types thereof) posited by the less parsimonious theory are explanatorily superfluous; rather, from the point of view of the less parsimonious theory, these entities (or types thereof) are indeed necessary to explain some of the evidence.

Consider, for example, the difference between Ptolemy's geocentric model of the solar system, on the one hand, and Copernicus's and Kepler's heliocentric models, on the other. Famously, the heliocentric models of Copernicus and especially Kepler involved postulating fewer epicycles than the geocentric model; indeed, these epicycles could eventually be eliminated entirely from the heliocentric model. This is often taken to be a paradigmatic case of parsimony influencing theory choice.[37] However, note that the argument we are

---

[36] More generally, it is a theorem of the probability axioms that if H_1 implies H_2 but not *vice versa*, then $Pr(H_1) < Pr(H_2)$.

[37] See, for example, Galileo (1632, 397) and Sober (2015, 12–22). With that said, one could also argue that the preference for the heliocentric model was due primarily to its superior syntactic simplicity, which seems to be Kuhn's (1977, 324) view, for instance.

currently considering cannot be used to explain the preference for the geocentric model in this case, since the geocentric model is clearly not identical to the heliocentric model except in that it posits some additional entities. For instance, the heliocentric model posits that all the planets revolve around the Sun; whereas the geocentric model posits that the Sun and the other planets revolve around the Earth. Relatedly, the geocentric model does not posit any entities that are explanatorily superfluous from its own point of view: Given the geocentric model's core commitment to placing the Earth at the center of the solar system, the various epicycles posited by that theory are all needed in order to explain astronomical observations such as the apparent retrograde motion of the other known planets (otherwise they would not have been posited in the first place!).

So if there is a general argument for the truth-conduciveness of parsimony, it cannot simply appeal to the supposed superfluousness of the entities (or types thereof) posited by less parsimonious theories. How then might a realist about explanatory goodness argue for their position regarding parsimony? As before, there are two main options here. The first is to argue on a priori grounds that more parsimonious theories are more likely to be true. In this vein, Swinburne (1997, 1) claims that the truth-conduciveness of parsimony is "an ultimate [i.e., fundamental] a priori principle" that cannot itself be justified by anything else (see also Biggs and Wilson, 2017). However, this claim is difficult to accept since, as van Fraassen (1989, 147–148) points out, to claim that more parsimonious theories are more likely to be true seems to involve an assumption that the world is more likely to contain fewer entities (or types thereof). That assumption is surely a contingent matter and so not something that could be ascertained a priori, but only (if at all) empirically.

The other option is to argue that parsimony is truth-conducive on that is, empirical, grounds. Such arguments generally appeal to a naturalistic methodology in which scientific practice itself is taken to be the best, if not the only, indication of what types of theories are more and less likely to be true (Baker, 2022, §4). In particular, some philosophers have suggested that scientists do in fact prefer more parsimonious theories, and that the general success of the scientific enterprise in getting at the truth suggests that this preference can be taken to be truth-conducive (Boyd, 1980; Burgess, 1998; Baker, 2007). Of course, antirealists might respond by suggesting that such an argument is question-begging, because by their lights we have little or no reason to think that the scientific enterprise is genuinely discovering the truth as opposed to, for example, merely increasing its capacity to generate instrumentally useful or empirically adequate theories (see, e.g., van Fraassen, 1980; Wray, 2018; Rowbottom, 2019).

Another line of objection to the naturalistic, *a posteriori*, strategy for arguing that parsimony is truth-conducive concerns whether scientists really do exhibit a general preference for more parsimonious theories. Salmon (2001, 81) notes that in some fields, such as anthropology and sociology, complex theories are actually preferred over parsimonious theories on the grounds that complex phenomena usually call for complex explanations (see also Day and Kincaid, 1994; Lange, 2022). Similar remarks have been made by Francis Crick, the biologist who discovered the helical structure of DNA along with James Watson. Crick suggests that while parsimony "is a useful tool in the physical sciences, it can be a very dangerous implement in biology" (Crick, 1988, 138). Finally, Baker (2007) considers cases from twentieth-century physics in which complexity seems to have been preferred over parsimony, on the grounds that if it's physically *possible* for an object to exist, then it (probably) *actually* exists. A case in point is Paul Dirac's consideration of the possible existence of magnetic "monopoles," that is, magnets with only one magnetic pole, within quantum mechanics. Dirac argued that because such monopoles can exist according to quantum mechanics, "one would be surprised if Nature had made no use of it" (Dirac, 1931, 71).

These cases suggest that although parsimony is sometimes taken to be truth-conducive by working scientists, sometimes the opposite of parsimony is taken to be truth-conducive. Note, however, that in either case scientists are assuming that there is a feature of the theory in question – namely, its parsimony *or lack thereof* – that can be used to gauge how likely the theory is to be true (cf. Lange, 2022, 97–98). Thus, there is a sense in which parsimony is still playing an important role in abductive reasoning in such cases; it's just that what is normally taken to be an explanatory "vice" now effectively functions as a virtue. Indeed, we can generalize this thought by noting that any theory can presumably be located on a scale from maximally to minimally parsimonious. In different circumstances, exactly where a theory is located on this scale could be taken to indicate how likely it is to be true. For example, one might think that, in certain domains, the correct explanations are most likely to exhibit a degree of parsimony that is, say, high but not maximal. In that case, what functions as an explanatory virtue could be not parsimony *simpliciter*, but rather how close to high-but-not-maximal-parsimony the relevant theories are.

In my view, this points the way towards a plausible view not just of parsimony, but of explanatory goodness in general, which in some ways transcends the realism/antirealism divide. We might call it *contextualism about explanatory goodness*. On this view, which features of a theory are truth-conducive depends on the "context," that is, on the phenomenon to be explained and our background beliefs about what sorts of explanations it most likely calls for.

These features could in principle be any readily-identifiable properties of a theory, but in actual science they tend to concern the extent to which the theory exhibits the explanatory virtues listed in Section 3.1, such as scope and parsimony. Importantly, however, *more* does not always imply *better*, for one's background beliefs about a particular phenomenon might suggest that the correct explanation exhibits only a moderate degree of scope, a low degree of parsimony, and so forth. If so, a theory with these characteristics should be considered the "best" explanation – the one to be preferred or inferred – even if another theory exhibits the explanatory virtues to a greater degree.

This is not the place to develop contextualism about explanatory goodness in any detail, but it is worth commenting on how it relates to realism about explanatory goodness. On my formulation, realism about some explanatory virtue holds that this virtue is truth-conducive, that is, that hypotheses which exhibit this virtue to a greater extent are more likely to be true, all other things being equal. Contextualism denies this, in that it holds that there is no linear or monotonic relationship between exhibiting the relevant virtue to a greater extent and being more likely to be true. For example, contextualism about parsimony may imply that, in certain contexts, a complex theory is likelier to be true than a parsimonious one. Nevertheless, contextualism – like realism – allows us to use explanatory virtues as a guide to truth, because the extent to which a given hypothesis does (or doesn't) exhibit explanatory virtues indicates, within a given context, how likely the hypothesis is to be true.

Let us take stock again. The explanatory virtue of parsimony is the extent to which a given hypothesis postulates fewer new entities, or types thereof. Realists regarding parsimony hold that it is an epistemic virtue, that is, that more parsimonious hypotheses are more likely to be true; whereas antirealists hold that parsimony is, at most, a merely pragmatic consideration. Some realists have argued that it is somehow a fundamental principle of rationality that more parsimonious theories are likelier to be true. However, this seems to conflict with the obvious fact that the universe could have contained a greater rather than lesser number of entities (or types thereof). Other realists have argued that scientists in fact prefer more parsimonious theories, and that the general success of accepted scientific theories indicates that this practice is in fact truth-conducive. However, an important counterpoint is that the preference for parsimonious theories appears not to be universal; rather, scientists sometimes prefer complex theories over more parsimonious ones. This suggest that the correct view of whether explanatory virtues track the truth is a "contextualist" one, according to which it depends on the context whether, and to what extent, a more parsimonious theory is more likely to be true than a more complex one.

4 Is Abductive Reasoning Irrational?

This section focuses on several challenges to the idea that abductive reasoning is or could be rational. These challenges differ from the concerns voiced in the previous section in that they target the structure of abductive reasoning rather than any substantive assumptions about whether better explaining theories are more likely to be true. In particular, these objections suggest that abductive reasoning – or at least some forms thereof – will lead reasoners to adopt attitudes that are either outright incoherent or highly implausible by their own lights.

4.1 The Bad Lot Objection

As mentioned briefly in Section 2, one of the most influential challenges to abductive reasoning is van Fraassen's *bad lot objection* to IBE. In van Fraassen's own memorable words:

> [Inference to the Best Explanation] is a rule that only selects the best among the historically given hypotheses. We can watch no contest of the theories we have so painfully struggled to formulate, with those no one has proposed. So our selection may well be the best of a bad lot (van Fraassen, 1989, 142–143).

The basic problem pointed out by van Fraassen here is that we may have no reason to think that any of the available explanatory hypotheses are true. The hypotheses that have been generated so far may all be false, in which case the correct explanation would be provided by a hypothesis outside of the set of available hypotheses. In that case, IBE would inevitably lead us to accept a false hypothesis, even if explanatory goodness tracks truth in a highly reliable manner, and even if we can reliably identify the best explaining hypothesis among those that are available at a given time.[38]

As it stands, van Fraassen's objection simply points to a conceptual possibility, namely that the true hypothesis may not have been made available. One might think that the mere possibility that abductive reasoning goes wrong in this way is not a strong argument against it, since any account of any form of nondeductive reasoning will readily acknowledge that such reasoning is fallible to some extent. However, in recent years van Fraassen's objection has been substantially bolstered by historical studies which suggest that working scientists sometimes find themselves in precisely the situation described by van Fraassen, in that every available theory about some phenomenon is, unbeknownst to them, false (e.g., Stanford, 2006; Wray, 2011; Kashyap, 2023).

---

[38] The bad lot objection is also sometimes called the *argument from underconsideration* (Lipton, 1993; Wray, 2008; Khalifa, 2010).

During the nineteenth century, for example, Charles Darwin, Francis Galton, and August Weisman each successively formulated and defended different false theories of the mechanism of biological heredity. Arguably, none of these theories provides as good an explanation of biological heredity as the chromosome theory of Boveri and Sutton, but the latter was not formulated until the early twentieth century. So Darwin, Galton, and Weisman were evidently working with a "bad lot" of explanatory hypotheses.[39]

This shows that the bad lot objection cannot be set aside as a mere conceptual possibility with no relevance for actual scientific practice. However, exactly what sort of problem the bad lot objection creates for abductive reasoning depends on what sort of account of abductive reasoning one endorses. In Section 2, we distinguished between *inferential, probabilistic,* and *hybrid* accounts of abductive reasoning. As noted then, van Fraassen originally conceived of the bad lot objection as targeting a specific sort of inferential account, namely IBE à la Harman (1965). Accordingly, most of the following discussion in this section focuses on how inferential accounts, such as IBE, might circumvent the bad lot objection. However, it is worth noting that the bad lot objection is also a problem for hybrid accounts in so far as these involve choosing an explanatory hypothesis among some set of available competing hypotheses – all of which may be false – even if this choice is ultimately meant to approximate a probabilistic evaluation of that hypothesis.

Indeed, at least some probabilistic accounts of abductive reasoning face a version of the bad lot objection that is no less difficult to handle than the original objection. In particular, consider what I called *Abductive Conditionalization –* which, recall, is a version of Bayesian Conditionalization in which the hypothesis H that best explains the evidence E is awarded a bonus probability *b*. Any application of Abductive Conditionalization presupposes that one has already formulated the hypothesis that in fact best explains E, since this is the hypothesis that is supposed to receive a bonus probability. Thus, if and in so far as one is uncertain about whether the hypothesis that best explains E has been formulated, one would not be in a position to add the bonus probability to any hypothesis (and subtract probability from other hypotheses – see §4.2). After all, any formulated hypothesis might be "the best of a bad lot" in the sense that it just provides the best explanation among a set of hypotheses that doesn't include the (as yet unformulated) hypothesis that in fact best explains E.[40]

---

[39] These examples of theories of biological heredity are discussed in great detail by Stanford (2006, chs. 3–5). It should be noted that Stanford is not focusing on IBE specifically, and that Stanford refers to the problem he is concerned with as the *Problem of Unconceived Alternatives* (for discussion, see, e.g., Magnus, 2010; Ruhmkorff, 2011; Egg, 2016; Dellsén, 2017d).

[40] A somewhat similar problem faces what I have called *constraining probabilistic accounts.* Recall that these accounts hold that hypotheses which provide better explanations should be

So, almost regardless of what sort of account of abductive reasoning one endorses, it is imperative to find some way or other of responding the bad lot objection. Dellsén (2017c) distinguishes between two different ways of doing so: *revisionary* and *reactionary* responses to the bad lot objection. According to revisionary responses, the bad lot objection should lead us to reformulate IBE, or replace it with some other account of abductive reasoning, so as to avoid or sidestep van Fraassen's objection. As we shall see below, this can be achieved in various ways, for example by adding some further conditions on the applicability of abductive reasoning or by weakening the form of the conclusion it is meant to warrant. According to reactionary responses, by contrast, there is no need for revising or replacing IBE in this way because the bad lot objection is, in one way or another, misguided or unpersuasive even when applied to the original form of IBE to which van Fraassen objected. In what follows, let us first consider two reactionary responses to the bad lot objection before turning to some revisionary responses.

The most influential reactionary response to the bad lot objection is due to Lipton (1993). As noted in Section 2, Lipton conceived of IBE as involving two temporally distinct stages: (i) the generation of a set of rival explanatory hypotheses, and (ii) the comparative evaluation of one of these hypotheses as providing the "best" explanation. Now, although steps (i) and (ii) are distinct, Lipton (1993, 96–99) suggests that someone who is capable of reliably comparing a set of explanatory hypotheses in step (ii) will also be capable of reliably generating the hypothesis that in fact provides the correct explanation in step (i). The reason for this, according to Lipton, is that in order to carry out a reliable comparative evaluation in step (ii), one must base that evaluation on a large set of true background theories, and these true background theories would themselves have to have been generated in a step (i) of an earlier application of IBE. So, says Lipton, one cannot consistently say that scientists are generally reliable at comparing explanatory hypotheses in step (ii) but not also reliable at generating true hypotheses in step (i).

---

assigned higher probabilities before one updates on the evidence. So, in particular, if H_2 is explanatorily better than H_1, one should assign a higher value to $Pr(H_2|E)$ than to $Pr(H_1|E)$. Now, if the best explanation of E is not yet formulated – call it H_x – then as a practical matter one obviously cannot assign any probability to that hypothesis given the evidence, $Pr(H_x|E)$. Consequently, it becomes unclear what probability one should assign even to H_1 or H_2 given E, because if some unformulated hypothesis H_x is to receive a greater share of the probability that is to be distributed among various competing hypotheses, then some other of these hypotheses – including, perhaps, H_1 and H_2, must receive a lesser share of that probability (see §4.2). So if one doesn't know whether there is some unformulated H_x that in fact provides the best explanation of one's evidence, then one doesn't know how to distribute probability even among the hypotheses that have been formulated.

One possible rejoinder to Lipton's response, on behalf of van Fraassen, is that van Fraassen never claimed that scientists are generally reliable at comparing explanatory hypotheses in step (ii). Although van Frassen never explicitly argued that scientists are unreliable at making such comparisons, he might take the bad lot objection, coupled with Lipton's response, to constitute an argument for that conclusion. However, as Lipton (1993, 98) in effect points out, this would seem to commit proponents of the bad lot objection to a much more radically skeptical position according to which we have little if any inductive powers at all. What made the bad lot objection interesting was that it seemed to undermine IBE, and to some extent abductive reasoning generally, even if scientists were granted the considerable inductive powers required to comparatively evaluate explanatory hypotheses in a reliable manner.

Another rejoinder to Lipton's response starts by noting that there is a perfectly good sense in which scientists may be reliable at comparative evaluations of theories even when their background theories are generally false.[41] By way of analogy, consider how a skilled logician may reliably accept only those conclusions that follow deductively from premises they also accept. Of course, the premises from which the logician deduces their conclusions may be false; still, there is a perfectly good sense in which the logician's inferences are reliable relative to the premises they accept. Similarly, scientists using IBE can be said to be reliable at making comparative evaluations to the extent that their evaluations reflect the weight of evidence for and against each hypothesis relative to the background theories they accept. If the background theories accepted by some scientists are false, then the relevant scientists may well be misled into ranking a false theory ahead of a true one. But this is no different from a logician who competently derives a false conclusion from false premises via a deductively valid argument. In both cases, there is a perfectly good sense in which the inference itself can be said to be reliable relative to the premises or background theories with which they started.

In light of this point, one can – contra Lipton – grant scientists considerable inductive powers regarding their reliability in comparatively evaluating explanatory hypotheses in stage (ii), and still maintain that we have little reason to think they are reliable at generating true explanatory hypotheses in stage (i). On this view, the relevant type of reliability is relative to the background theories on which they largely base their evaluations: if these theories are generally

---

[41] See Dellsén (2017c, 35–36) for a more detailed consideration of two possible senses in which scientists' comparative evaluations may be said to be reliable, and how this affects Lipton's argument.

true, then scientists will reliably rank true theories above false ones; if their background theories are generally false, they may well fail to do so in many or most cases. To illustrate with a concrete case, consider that in the early nineteenth century, Alfred Wegener's theory of continental drift was rejected in favor of a theory on which the continents had fixed locations, partly because the geophysical theories that were accepted at the time strongly indicated that it would be impossible for the continents to move around as rapidly as Wegener's theory predicted. There is a perfectly good sense in which a reliable ranking of the two theories places the fixed-continents theory above Wegener's theory relative to such background theories. In that same sense, reliable rankers of the two theories would then reverse the ranking in the late 1950s, when the relevant geophysical theories had been overturned so as to allow for much more rapid movements of the tectonic plates which had then been discovered to undergird continental drift (Bowler and Morus, 2005, 237–252).

Although other reactionary responses to the bad lot objection have been developed and defended,[42] let us now move on to consider revisionary responses instead. The most concessive sort of revisionary response would hold that since we have formulated only a limited range of explanatory hypotheses, the conclusion of an abductive inference can at most be that one of these hypotheses is epistemically superior to the other hypotheses that have been formulated so far. Put differently, abductive reasoning would not really warrant inferring that any explanatory hypothesis is true (or even probably and/or approximately true); only that a hypothesis is superior to the other hypotheses that have been formulated at a given time. For example, Kuipers (2000) develops an inferential account of abductive reasoning on which the conclusion of such reasoning is only that a given hypothesis is *closer to the truth* (i.e., more truthlike) than its available competitors. In a similar vein, Dellsén (2018) argues that in many circumstances abductive reasoning only warrants inferring that a given hypothesis is *more likely to be true* than its available competitors, but that this generally suffices for reasonably accepting it as a working hypothesis in one's subsequent investigations.[43]

However, these revisionary responses – by themselves – may well concede too much to the bad lot objection, for there are surely *some* cases in which

---

[42] See Lipton (1993, 94–96), Schupbach (2014), and Shaffer (2021). For rejoinders to some of these responses, see Wray (2008), Khalifa (2010), and Dellsén (2017c).

[43] For similar reasons, various authors have argued that the attitude we should take towards an explanatory hypothesis we end up with should not be one of belief at all – not even belief that the hypothesis is probably and/or approximately true. Rather, according to these authors, we should end up tentatively accepting or pursuing the hypothesis in our future research (Kapitan, 1992; Dawes, 2013; Nyrup, 2015; Cabrera, 2017; although see also Henderson, 2022).

abductive reasoning can be used to establish not merely the comparative conclusion that a given hypothesis is closer to the truth, or more likely to be true, than its competitors, but also the absolute conclusion that the hypothesis is close to the truth or probably true. After all, we often rely on the probable and/or approximate truth of various theories for certain purposes, such as in predictions and explanations, and merely knowing that a theory is better than currently available competitors is often not good enough for such purposes. For example, the major policy recommendations that are grounded in the theory of anthropogenic global warming (i.e., the claim that human activities are a significant causal factor in global temperature increases since the industrial revolution) are evidently not based on the (comparative) conclusion that this theory is epistemically superior to its available competitors. Rather, it is based on the (absolute) conviction that this theory is almost certainly true, or at least sufficiently close to the truth so as to warrant the relevant policy recommendations.

To deal with this concern, some philosophers have suggested that IBE should be modified so as to include an additional clause requiring that the inferred explanatory hypothesis not only be better than available competitors, but also "good enough" (e.g., Musgrave, 1988; Lipton, 2004). In other words, these philosophers suggest that IBE should be taken to involve not just a comparative evaluation in which some set of available hypotheses are compared to each other in terms of their explanatory goodness, but also an absolute evaluation of whether the best of these hypotheses is a sufficiently good explanation to be inferred at all. This is supposed to address the bad lot objection because in situations where none of the available explanatory hypotheses are true, even the best available explanatory hypotheses might be thought to be insufficiently good to be inferred by this criterion.

One issue with this response is that it is far from clear what the above authors mean when they say that an explanation must be "good enough." The most natural interpretation of the phrase is that the inferred hypothesis must exceed some designated threshold of explanatory goodness, where "explanatory goodness" is understood in absolute rather than merely comparative terms. On this view, each hypothesis is associated with some level of explanatory goodness relative to the evidence at a given time, and whether the hypothesis counts as providing a "good enough" explanation simply depends on whether that level exceeds a threshold. However, Dellsén (2021, 161–164) argues that adding such a clause to IBE leads to various new problems, and is anyway ill-suited to address the original bad lot objection. Consider, for example, the many cases in which scientists have accepted some explanatory hypothesis at an earlier time, only to later reject it in favor of a newly-formulated alternative that provides an even better explanation of the relevant evidence (Sklar, 1981; Stanford, 2006). In such cases, the scientists must have assumed that even the earlier hypothesis exceeded the threshold for explanatory goodness – otherwise, they would hardly have accepted it – and yet the relevant hypothesis turned out to be false by our current lights. So, in these cases, having a hypothesis that exceeds the threshold for explanatory goodness evidently did prevent scientists from inferring from a "bad lot" of explanatory hypotheses.

In view of such problems, Dellsén (2021, 164–172) develops a quite different account of when, and why, the best available explanatory hypothesis can be considered "good enough" to be inferred. In short, the best available explanatory hypothesis can be inferred when it has been through a temporally extended process which Dellsén calls *explanatory consolidation*. This process consists in the accumulation of two quite different types of information which gradually make it more plausible that the hypothesis one tentatively accepts indeed provides a better explanation of one's evidence than any other hypothesis that could be formulated. Specifically, as *empirical evidence* for the hypothesis accumulates, it gradually increases the plausibility that no alternative to it could explain all that evidence in an equally satisfactory manner. In addition, repeated *unsuccessful attempts to formulate* alternative hypotheses that provide better explanations also increase the plausibility that the tentatively accepted hypothesis cannot be matched in that regard (Dawid et al., 2015; Dellsén, 2017d). If all goes well, then eventually we will have accumulated enough information of these two types so as to make it exceedingly plausible that the hypothesis in question is "good enough" to be inferred.

4.2 The Dynamic Dutch Book Argument

Thus far we have considered an objection to abductive reasoning, the bad lot objection, which primarily targets inferential accounts, such as Harman's and Lipton's IBE. Recall from Section 2 that van Fraassen takes this objection to motivate a move away from inferential accounts towards a certain sort of probabilistic account, but that van Fraassen goes on to argue that this probabilistic account should be rejected as well. In this section, we will take a closer look at this second argument of van Fraassen's, and consider some recent responses to it.

Recall that van Fraassen argues that in order for abductive reasoning to have a place within Bayesianism, the hypothesis that best explains some evidence E must be awarded greater personal probability than the Bayesian framework would, by itself, confer on the hypothesis. In particular, van Fraassen suggests that this would require a modification of Bayesian Conditionalization such that a bonus is added to the posterior probability an agent assigns to the hypothesis that provides the best explanation of the newly obtained evidence. In Section 2, we called this general idea *Abductive Conditionalization*, and noted that a simple version of it would require agents to set their new probability in a hypothesis H to $Pr'(H) = Pr(H|E) + b$, where b is the bonus probability awarded to H for best explaining E. Note that if H is awarded a bonus in this way, then at least some rival hypotheses must receive a penalty so as to balance the total probability awarded to H and its mutually exclusive and jointly exhaustive rivals (more on this below).

Van Fraassen's (1989, 160–170) objection to Abductive Conditionalization is, in brief, that because it conflicts with Bayesian Conditionalization in assigning a bonus to some hypotheses that wouldn't receive it according to Bayesian Conditionalization, it is undermined by any positive argument in favor of the latter. In particular, van Fraassen appeals to the so-called *dynamic Dutch book argument* in favor of Bayesian Conditionalization. In a nutshell, this argument says that any agent who updates their personal probabilities when they receive new evidence via any rule that conflicts with Bayesian Conditionalization will be such that, if someone (a "Dutch bookie") were to offer them a particular series of monetary bets at different times that are all fair by the agent's lights at each time,[44] then the agent would be guaranteed to lose money no matter what the outcomes of the bets would be. Indeed, the agent would be able to know all this beforehand – that by following the alternative rule for how to update their probabilities (e.g., Abductive Conditionalization) they can only end up losing money on bets they consider fair when the bets are offered. According to van Fraassen, this indicates that the agent is guilty of a kind of irrationality over time, often referred to as *diachronic incoherence*. Since Abductive Conditionalization clearly conflicts with Bayesian Conditionalization by virtue of adding a bonus probability to some hypotheses (and having others incur a corresponding penalty), Abductive Conditionalization would necessarily be an irrational way to update one's credences in light of new evidence, according to van Fraassen.[45]

As noted in Section 2, many proponents of probabilistic accounts of abductive reasoning agree with van Fraassen that it would be a bad idea to assign bonus probabilities to the best explaining hypotheses in the way suggested

---

[44] A "fair" bet is one that has an expected value of zero given the agent's personal probabilities, that is, roughly such that the agent can expect to break even in the long run if she repeatedly made the same bet.

[45] See also Pettigrew (2021) for a version of this argument that doesn't appeal to rational betting behavior, but instead argues that using Bayesian Conditionalization (rather than Abductive Conditionalization) maximizes the expected accuracy of one's credences.

by Abductive Conditionalization. They instead argue that explanatory considerations should play some other role in the assignment of probabilities to hypotheses (see §2.3). With that said, however, one of the more influential proponents of abductive reasoning, Igor Douven, has put up a vigorous defense of Abductive Conditionalization in a number of recent publications (e.g., Douven, 2013, 2017, 2022; Douven and Wenmackers, 2017). In particular, Douven formulates a version of Abductive Conditionalization in which the bonus probability added to the hypothesis that best explains the evidence is balanced out by a general penalty to all other hypotheses. With some slight simplifications, this rule can be formulated as follows (see Douven, 2022, 51):

EXPL: Let $\mathcal{H} = \{H_1, ..., H_n\}$ be a set of mutually exclusive and jointly exhaustive hypotheses, and let f be a function that assigns a positive value b to the hypothesis in $\mathcal{H}$ that best explains E, and 0 to all other hypotheses therein.[46] Then an abductive reasoner should update their credence in any hypothesis H_j by setting:

$$Pr'(H_j) = \frac{Pr(H_j)\,Pr(E|H_j) + f(H_j, E, \mathcal{H})}{\sum_{k=1}^{n}(Pr(H_k)\,Pr(E|H_k) + f(H_k, E, \mathcal{H}))}$$

Although EXPL may seem complicated, the intuitive thought behind it is quite simple: The hypothesis in $\mathcal{H}$ that best explains E gets a bonus probability, and all other hypotheses in $\mathcal{H}$ are penalized in proportion to how probable they would have been without these penalties.

The crux of Douven's defense of EXPL (and to some extent Abductive Conditionalization in general) is that even if EXPL would render one vulnerable to a guaranteed loss in the situations described in the dynamic Dutch book argument, it does not follow that using EXPL rather than Bayesian Conditionalization is irrational *all things considered*. Rather, vulnerability to dynamic Dutch books may just be a small downside to EXPL which may be outweighed by other considerations that count in its favor and against Bayesian Conditionalization. In support of this, one might point out that the situations described in the dynamic Dutch book argument are extremely rare, so the sort of irrationality that the argument supposedly brings out in agents updating by EXPL might be thought to be relatively harmless. Thus, if there are important benefits

---

[46] Formally, the function f is characterized as follows:

$$f(H_j, E, \mathcal{H}) = \begin{cases} b & \text{if } H_j \text{ best explains E} \\ 0 & \text{otherwise} \end{cases}$$

to using EXPL rather than Bayesian Conditionalization, then vulnerability to dynamic Dutch books may well be a small price to pay, all things considered.

Douven (2022, ch. 4) argues that there are indeed such benefits to using EXPL rather than good old Bayesian Conditionalization. Douven shows that, in various computer simulations in which artificial agents are attempting to discover a coin's bias by flipping it repeatedly, agents who use EXPL tend to converge on true hypotheses much faster than those who use Bayesian Conditionalization. Here, "convergence" is a matter of assigning a probability above a high threshold, for example 0.9 or 0.99. So, according to Douven, users of EXPL will be in a position to accept or assert true hypotheses more quickly, and more often, than those who simply use Bayesian Conditionalization – at least if a hypothesis' acceptability and/or assertability is a matter of it having a high probability (see, e.g., Foley, 1992; Douven, 2006). As Douven acknowledges, however, EXPL also tends to lead agents to assign higher probabilities to false hypotheses more often than Bayesian Conditionalization. Overall, then, one might say that EXPL is simply riskier than Bayesian Conditionalization, but that the risk may often be worth taking.

Apart from defending EXPL against van Fraassen's Dutch book argument in this way, Douven (2022, chs. 6–7) also gives a related positive argument for EXPL which appeals to the notion of *ecological rationality* (Gigerenzer, 2000). The idea, roughly, is that how it is rational for someone to behave – or, in this case, how it is rational for them to update their personal probabilities – may depend not only on facts about the agent's psychology but also on facts about the environment or situation they find themselves in. Douven again appeals to computer simulations to suggest that from this perspective it may be better to use EXPL than other updating rules, including Bayesian Conditionalization, in a variety of circumstances – including situations in which agents update not only on ordinary empirical evidence but also on the opinions of their peers (see also Douven and Wenmackers, 2017).

A possible limitation of Douven's approach concerns whether EXPL can be extended beyond the simple coin tossing cases in this simulations. As formulated above, EXPL gives a probability bonus to the hypothesis that *best explains* the evidence, but nothing is said explicitly about what counts as "best explaining." In Douven's coin tossing simulations, the "best explainer" is simply the available hypothesis that comes closest to postulating a bias that exactly matches the observed frequency thus far. For example, if the available hypotheses posit biases at 10% intervals (0%, 10%, 20%, etc.), and 681 out of 1,000 tosses have landed heads thus far, then the "best explainer" is the hypothesis that the coin is 70% biased in favor of heads (Douven, 2013, 432). This is clear enough for hypotheses about how a coin is biased, but what about more realistic cases in which either the evidence or the hypotheses – or indeed both – do not themselves concern probabilistic quantities like frequencies or chances that can be so easily compared quantitively?

In such cases, EXPL will need to appeal to some other criteria for what counts as the "best explainer" among available hypotheses, such as explanatory virtues like scope and simplicity. However, it remains to be seen whether EXPL, when coupled with such criteria for what counts as the best explanation, would indeed have the epistemic benefits Douven argues it has in simple coin tossing situations. Furthermore, EXPL may have more serious epistemic drawbacks in more realistic cases than in coin tossing situations, because in such cases there may not be enough obtainable evidence to turn around assignments of high probabilities to false hypotheses. After all, working scientists are not often in a situation in which they can simply toss a coin to obtain more evidence pertinent to a given hypothesis; rather, they often have to design and run entirely new experiments, or engage in laborious field-work, in order to collect any new evidence worth speaking of.

4.3 Recent Challenges to Abductive Reasoning

Van Fraassen's two challenges to the rationality of abductive reasoning, the bad lot objection and the dynamic Dutch book argument, are without question the most influential problems of this sort in the literature. In recent years, however, abductive reasoning has been challenged in other ways as well. In this final section, we will briefly look at some of these more recent challenges and how proponents of various accounts of abductive reasoning might respond.

4.3.1 The Screening-Off Challenge

One recent challenge concerns the issue of whether there is a role for abductive reasoning within Bayesianism. As we have seen, most proponents of probabilistic and hybrid accounts of abductive reasoning argue, in different ways, that abductive reasoning is not only compatible with, but indeed complements, the Bayesian approach to scientific reasoning. This contention is called into question by William Roche and Elliott Sober's *screening-off challenge*.

Roche and Sober (2013) suggest that in order for explanatory considerations to count as *evidentially relevant* within the Bayesian approach, the fact that some hypothesis H explains some evidence E – call that fact X (for eXplanation) – must raise the probability of H more than E would do all by itself: $Pr(H|E\&X) > Pr(H|E)$. Conversely, according to Roche and Sober, explanatory considerations would be *evidentially irrelevant* if $Pr(H|E\&X) = Pr(H|E)$ – that is, if E "screens off" H from X. In support of this criterion, Roche and

Sober point out that if conditionalizing on X does not raise or otherwise alter the probability of H given E in this way, then there is apparently no need for the Bayesian to appeal to explanatory considerations in spelling out how much some evidence confirms some hypothesis. Any probability added by the discovery of X (i.e., the fact that H explains E) has already been taken into account when E raised the probability of H. Roche and Sober then go on to argue, with the use of a suggestive case study, that the equality $Pr(H|E\&X) = Pr(H|E)$ does indeed hold.

Roche and Sober's argument has led to a flurry of responses. One response disputes that the equality $Pr(H|E\&X) = Pr(H|E)$ holds either in Roche and Sober's own case study or in other similar cases of abductive reasoning (Climenhaga, 2017a; see also Roche and Sober, 2017). A much more common set of responses challenge the idea that Roche and Sober's *screening-off criterion*, $Pr(H|E\&X) = Pr(H|E)$, is an appropriate criterion for evidential irrelevance. For example, McCain and Poston (2014) argue that explanatory considerations are evidentially relevant in that they affect how resilient one's personal probabilities are to being changed when new evidence is obtained (see also Roche and Sober, 2014; McCain and Poston, 2018).[47]

Indeed, looking back at the accounts of abductive reasoning surveyed in Section 2, including the various probabilistic accounts thereof, it is not clear whether or how Roche and Sober's screening-off challenge undermines any of these accounts – even though each such account is surely spelling out a sense in which explanation would be evidentially relevant. For example, $Pr(H|E\&X) = Pr(H|E)$ is consistent with the central idea behind constraining probabilistic accounts, according to which explanatory considerations go into determining the value one should assign to $Pr(H|E)$ in the first place – and perhaps therefore also to $Pr(H|E\&X)$. On these accounts, had H not explained E, then the value one should assign to $Pr(H|E)$ – and thus, perhaps, to $Pr(H|E\&X)$ as well – would have been lower than it actually is. That is surely an important sense in which explanation is evidentially relevant, but it is perfectly consistent with $Pr(H|E\&X) = Pr(H|E)$.[48]

---

[47] For another argument that explanatory considerations might be evidentially relevant in other ways, see Lange (2017); see also Roche and Sober (2019) and Lange (2020, 2023).

[48] In response to this criticism, Roche and Sober might reply that they only meant to suggest that *there is a sense in which* explanatoriness is evidentially irrelevant, and that the screening-off criterion captures this sense (Roche and Sober, 2017, 582n1). But this invites the follow-up objection that Roche and Sober's criterion is so divorced from the accounts of abductive reasoning in the literature that their screening-off challenge fails to undermine any of these accounts. In order for Roche and Sober's argument to hit home, they would need to show that the screening-off criterion of explanatory irrelevance has been, or should be, accepted by proponents of abductive reasoning.

4.3.2 The Problem of Multiple Plausible Rivals

Another recent challenge to abductive reasoning concerns the fact that in many accounts of abductive reasoning, one infers or probabilistically prefers only the hypothesis that provides the very best explanation of the evidence, even though there may be many quite plausible competing hypotheses that provide nearly as good explanations. Dellsén (2017a) calls this *the problem of multiple rivals*.[49]

Consider situations in which there are multiple available explanatory hypotheses, $H_1, \ldots, H_n$, each of which provides what is intuitively a fairly good explanation of the evidence E as compared to the hypothesis H_i that *best* explains E. In cases of this sort, the sheer number of plausible alternative hypotheses to H_i would seem to undermine the rationality of inferring, via IBE or any similar inferential or hybrid account of abductive reasoning, that H_i is indeed true.[50] Consider, for example, that the best explanation for the origin of life on Earth is arguably the so-called RNA world hypothesis, according to which life began with the formation of self-replicating RNA molecules. However, there are several other plausible alternative explanations, most of which claim that life began with the formation of some nucleic acid or other – although they disagree about which type of nucleic acid (PNA, TNA, or GNA). Here, the availability of so many plausible rival explanatory hypotheses seem to undermine any inference to one of these hypotheses, including the RNA world hypothesis.

How should advocates of abductive reasoning respond to this problem?[51] Dellsén (2017a, 24–28) suggests that proponents of inferential and hybrid accounts, such as IBE, may deal with this problem by moving to a generalization of IBE that he calls *abductively robust inference* (ARI). The basic idea appeals to the fact that a claim C may be entailed by *several* of the hypotheses that provide some of the best explanations of the evidence, so that if any of these hypotheses is true (regardless of which of one), C would be true. A bit more precisely, suppose C is entailed by all of the k hypotheses that provide the best k explanations of the evidence, where k is some natural number (less than or possibly equal to the number of available hypotheses n). For a

---

[49] McCain and Poston (2019) discuss a closely related challenge, which they dub *the disjunction objection*, and which they attribute to brief remarks made by van Fraassen (1989) and Fumerton (1995).

[50] Indeed, it would also seem to undermine the rationality of assigning a higher probability only to H_i, and therefore assigning lower probabilities to at least some of its rival hypotheses, as per Douven's EXPL (see §4.2).

[51] McCain and Poston (2019) suggest that their version of the problem, that is the disjunction objection, can be avoided by adding a clause to IBE requiring that the best explanation must also be "good enough." Dellsén (2017a, 24) anticipates this type of response and argues that it doesn't work as a solution to the problem of plausible rivals.

large enough k, C may then be confidently inferred even if none of the available explanatory hypotheses $H_1, \ldots, H_n$ – including the very best explanatory hypothesis H_i. After all, each one of $H_1, \ldots, H_n$ would be subject to the problem of multiple rivals, whereas C would not be subject to any such problem; on the contrary, the multiplicity of plausible rivals all of which entail C arguably strengthens the support for C, for it shows that C is "robust" across the various explanatory possibilities described by each rival hypothesis (Woodward, 2006). Returning to our example of hypotheses about the origin of life, note that the four best alternative explanations for the origin of life all posit that life began with the formation of some type of nucleic acid – be it RNA, PNA, TNA, or GNA (i.e., by an xNA). According to the version of ARI where $k = 4$, we can thus confidently infer this "robust" result can be inferred.

A fair complaint about ARI is that it is underspecified in some important respects. Indeed, Dellsén (2017a, 26) emphasizes that ARI is not in fact an inference rule at all, but a *pattern* of multiple such rules for different values of k. Setting a higher value to k will generally make the resulting inference rule *epistemically safer*, in that one will be less likely to infer something false, but also *less powerful*, in that the inferred claim C will generally have to be a logically weaker proposition. Since one may want to balance safety and power differently in different circumstances, for example depending on how much is at stake, different instantiations of ARI (i.e., different values for k) may be appropriate in different circumstances. In this respect, ARI should arguably be left unspecified so that it instead preserves the flexibility required to balance safety and power in different ways.[52] With that said, there are other aspects of ARI that arguably need to be spelled out in greater detail. For example, in some cases one might want to allow an inference to a claim C that is merely entailed by *most* – rather than *all* – of the k hypotheses that provide the best explanations of the evidence. Furthermore, in those cases, it surely also matters *how good an explanation* is provided by each of the hypotheses that entail C. More work is needed to flesh out ARI along these dimensions.

4.3.3 Incoherence Across Explanatory Levels

A third and final recent challenge to abductive reasoning concerns the fact that a given phenomenon can often be explained at multiple "levels." Climenhaga (2017b) argues that this makes some influential accounts of abductive reasoning *incoherent*, in that these accounts will imply that agents should make inferences or probability assignments that are incompatible with one another.

---

[52] It is worth noting that when we set $k = 1$, we get an inference rule that is extensionally equivalent to IBE. It is in this sense that ARI is a generalization of IBE (Dellsén, 2017a, 27).

Consider, in particular, a standard version of IBE which holds that one may infer a hypothesis just in case it provides a better explanation of one's evidence than any other competing hypothesis. Now, at least in some cases, it seems that this idea implies that one can infer several different hypotheses from the same evidence, because the evidence can be explained at different "levels" such that the inferred hypotheses do not compete with each other but only with other hypotheses at the same "level." In particular, suppose that, at one "level" of explanation, H_a provides the best explanation of some evidence E; while at another "level," H_b provides the best explanation; and yet H_a and H_b are incompatible propositions. If such cases are possible, the upshot seems to be that IBE, at least as it is standardly formulated, recommends inferring two incompatible propositions, H_a and H_b.

Climenhaga (2017b, 253–254) demonstrates that such cases are possible by considering a rather artificial setup involving several urns containing differently colored balls and coin flips that determine which of these an agent randomly chooses balls from. To see the relevance of Climenhaga's problem to scientific practice, let us examine a more realistic case instead. Consider the fact that both birds and Pterygota (i.e., flying insects) are able to fly. Why is that? At a certain abstract level of explanation, there are two relevant explanatory hypotheses to consider, namely that the ability to fly is a trait inherited from a common flying ancestor, on the one hand, and that it isn't, on the other. The latter type of explanation – that the ability to fly was not present in the common ancestor of birds and Pterygota and instead evolved independently in the lineage of each – would be an instance of what evolutionary biologists call *convergent evolution*. We thus have the following two explanatory hypotheses:

(I) Flight evolved convergently in birds and Pterygota.
(II) Birds and Pterygota share a common flying ancestor.

So which explanation is better, (I) or (II)? When considered at this level of abstraction, it's plausible that (II) would provide the better explanation, at least all other things being equal. To see why, note that (II) would require only a single mutation (or, perhaps more plausibly, a single *series* of mutations) to have occurred from a nonflying species to a flying species, namely one that occurred before the lineage of birds and Pterygota split into different branches. By contrast, (I) would require two mutations (or two unrelated *series* of mutations), one in the lineage between the common ancestor and birds and another between the common ancestor and Pterygota. There is thus a clear sense in which (II) is more parsimonious. Perhaps relatedly, it seems considerably more likely that random events such as the particular type of mutation required to obtain the ability to fly would happen only once rather than twice.[53] Assuming that being the best explanation has something to do with being more parsimonious and/or conferring greater probability on the evidence, this might lead us to conclude that (II) rather than (I) should be inferred via IBE.

However, we may also consider this issue from the point of view of somewhat more detailed explanatory hypotheses. In particular, let us suppose that we are interested in learning not only about whether birds and Pterygota share a common flying ancestor, but also when (if at all) there were evolutionary pressures to evolve the ability to fly. So consider the following four explanatory hypotheses concerning how exactly birds and Pterygota evolved which take a stand on this issue as well:

(1) Flight evolved convergently in birds and Pterygota, and there were similar evolutionary pressures favoring flight in the lineages of both.
(2) Flight evolved convergently in birds and Pterygota, and there were dissimilar evolutionary pressures favoring flight in the lineage of each.
(3) Birds and Pterygota share a common flying ancestor, and there were similar evolutionary pressures favoring flight in the lineages of both.
(4) Birds and Pterygota share a common flying ancestor, and there were dissimilar evolutionary pressures favoring flight in the lineage of each.

Given *this* partition of the explanatory hypotheses, one could very well argue that the best explanation is (1). After all, if there were indeed similar evolutionary pressures favoring flight among the ancestors of birds and insects respectively, then one should expect flight to evolve in both lineages independently (i.e., convergently). Indeed, (1) is the hypothesis that is generally accepted in contemporary evolutionary biology, for various reasons that need not concern us here. So let's suppose – if only for the sake of the argument – that out of (1)–(4), (1) should be inferred via IBE.

The problem now is that the two explanations that we have concluded should both be inferred via IBE from the same fact are logically incompatible. If flight evolved convergently, as per (1), then birds and Pterygota do not share a common ancestor, contrary to (II). Apparently, then, IBE warrants inferences to logically incompatible claims. One could of course maintain that there is nothing wrong with accepting incompatible claims in some cases – as when one accepts both general relativity and quantum mechanics despite the apparent incompatibility between these theories – and that this would just be another case of that sort. However, all other things being equal, it is arguably at least a

---

[53] This is a point nicely made by Sober (1994), whose discussion of similar cases from evolutionary biology is my inspiration for this example.

downside to IBE if it leads so easily to incompatible conclusions. Furthermore, this concession would seem to conflict with scientific practice, such as in the case above, because evolutionary biologists do not generally accept both (1) and (II); rather, they accept only (1).

A potential solution to Climenhaga's problem starts from noting that there is an important asymmetry between the two sets of competing explanations listed above. The hypotheses in the first set, (I)–(II), are strictly less informative than the hypotheses in the second set, (1)–(4). After all, each hypothesis in the second set entails a hypothesis in the first but not *vice versa*. For instance, (1) entails (I) but (I) does not entail (1). Indeed, (I) is equivalent to the disjunction of (1) and (2), while (II) is in turn equivalent to the disjunction of (3) and (4). So, from the point of view of those who advance (1)–(4), (I) and (II) are *incomplete* explanations: They fail to take a stand on the arguably crucial issue of whether there were similar or dissimilar evolutionary pressures that led to flight in both birds and Pterygota. No similar charge can be levelled at (1)–(4) from the point of view of those who advance (I) and (II), since there is no issue on which latter, but not the former, take a stand.

Based on these considerations, one might then suggest that there is a privileged "level" of explanation on which IBE should be taken to operate – at least in the type of cases that lead to incompatible claims being inferred via IBE. In short, the privileged "level" is that at which the set of hypotheses provide more informative explanations. In the choice between the two sets of hypotheses considered above, IBE should therefore operate on (1)–(4), and so arguably warrant inferring (1). And since (1) entails (I), there is a sense in which (I) can also be inferred via IBE, albeit indirectly. After all, anyone who is in a position to infer (1) is also clearly in a position to infer an immediate logical consequence thereof, namely (II). Dellsén (2016) refers to this variation on standard IBE as *indirect IBE*, and suggests that in it one infers a hypothesis H in virtue of H being entailed by a stronger hypothesis H* that explains E better than any competing explanatory hypothesis.[54] The point, then, is not that no hypothesis from the set (I)–(II) can be inferred via IBE, but rather that (I) rather than (II) should be inferred because (I) is, whereas (II) is not, part of the best complete explanation, namely (1).

---

[54] Indeed, Dellsén (2016, 224) argues that it is common among proponents of IBE to implicitly count these types of inferences as instances of IBE. For example, Harman (1965, 90–91) suggests that, from the fact that all observed As have been Bs, one may infer that the next observed A will be also be a B. However, the next observed A being B clearly does not explain why all observed As have been Bs; rather, what explains the latter is (on Harman's view) that all As are Bs, from which one can then deduce that the next observed A will be a B (see also Lipton, 2004, 63–64).

Conclusion

Where does all of this leave us? I hope it's clear at this point that both the general term "abductive reasoning," and the popular slogan "Inference to the Best Explanation," tend to mean different things to different philosophers. Often prompted by various challenges to the cogency of abductive reasoning, these philosophers have responded by clarifying, refining, or developing their accounts of abductive reasoning so as to meet these challenges. Throughout this Element, I have often indicated my favored approach to meeting each challenge, but only in a piecemeal manner. In this brief final section, I wish to sketch a more holistic picture of how the pieces hang together in my view.

As discussed in Section 2, a crucial issue is whether one's account takes abductive reasoning to be inferential, probabilistic, or some hybrid of both. As I indicated already in that section, I favor a version of the third type of account, on which a form of abductive inference serves as a heuristic for rational probability assignments in which a preference for better explaining theories emerges naturally (see §2.4). In my view, this heuristic account of abductive reasoning provides us with "the best of both worlds," in that we can draw upon the powerful probabilistic machinery of the Bayesian framework to account for ideally rational reasoning in science, while still preserving a place for a the type of comparative explanatory evaluation that seems to make up much of the actual reasoning that goes on in science. Of course, in combining elements from inferential and probabilistic accounts, this heuristic account opens itself up to the challenges facing both. In my view, however, these challenges can be met.

The most important challenge to probabilistic accounts is arguably the dynamic Dutch book argument (see §4.2). However, this argument only applies to probabilistic accounts that involve some alternative updating rule to Bayesian Conditionalization, such as what I have called Abductive Conditionalization. In my view, however, the kinds of probabilistic accounts to which the heuristic account should appeal are not committed to Abductive Conditionalization, and instead either claim that preferences for hypotheses that better explain *emerge* from the probabilistic machinery given assumptions about the natural distribution of prior probabilities, or that explanatory considerations *constrain* which initial probability assignments are rational (see §2.3). These accounts are also not vulnerable to any form of the *screening-off challenge*, since neither type of account holds that abductive reasoning works by updating on a specific explanatory proposition that the rest of our evidence "screens off" (see §4.3.1). Thus if the heuristic account is coupled with probabilistic accounts of these "emergent" or "constraining" varieties, then I see little reason to worry about these challenges.

The most prominent challenge to inferential accounts is the bad lot objection (see §4.1). In my view, that challenge cannot be met within the confines of Harman's (1965) original notion of Inference to the Best Explanation, or Lipton's (2004) influential development thereof. Accordingly, I believe we need a more sophisticated account of the type of *inference* involved in abductive reasoning on the heuristic account thereof. Specifically, we should acknowledge, firstly, that the process of abductive reasoning is rarely complete once a hypothesis has been identified as the one which provides the best explanation of those that have been generated. Although such a hypothesis may be tentatively adopted as a working hypothesis, we often want – and sometimes need – greater assurance that this hypothesis is not *merely* the best we have thought of so far, but also quite likely true (or approximately so). In those cases, I have suggested that scientists ought to – and normally *do* – go through a process of *explanatory consolidation*, in which accumulating evidence and failed attempts to formulate better alternatives gradually make the hypothesis more plausible (see §4.1). Secondly, we should also acknowledge that abductive reasoning need not always warrant inferring the entirety of the hypothesis that provides the best explanation of the evidence. In some cases – especially when there are multiple plausible rival explanations on the table – abductive reasoning may only warrant inferring a weaker claim that is entailed not only by the very best explanation, but also by some or all of the other reasonably good explanations that are available (see §4.3.2).

Apart from the various challenges that face inferential, probabilistic, and hybrid accounts, there is also the more general challenge of why we should prefer "better explanations" at all. For example, why prefer theories that explain more to those that explain less, or more parsimonious theories to complex ones? As discussed in Section 3, philosophers are divided roughly between realists about explanatory goodness, who hold that better explanations are more likely to be true, and antirealists, who hold that better explanations are (at best) more convenient to work with. Moreover, realists disagree amongst themselves on whether providing better explanations can be shown a priori, or instead a posteriori, to be truth-conducive (see §3.2). My own position on this thorny issue is that different approaches may be appropriate for different explanatory virtues, and that at least some of the virtues – for example, parsimony – may be truth-tracking in some contexts but not others. In my view, this is not a problem for the heuristic account of abductive reasoning that I favor, since abductive reasoners can – and often *do* – choose not to appeal to the relevant virtues in the contexts in which they fail to be truth-tracking (see §§3.3–3.4).

In summary, then, the overall account of abductive reasoning that I favor is a combination of several complementary theses, the most central of which are the following:

(i) For some explanatory virtues, such as scope, probabilistic preferences for more virtuous theories emerge naturally in ideally rational Bayesian reasoners whose prior probabilities satisfy plausible constraints.

(ii) For other explanatory virtues, such as parsimony, context determines the extent to which theories that possess them are probabilistically preferred or dispreferred by ideally rational Bayesian agents.

(iii) In either case, the extent to which an explanatory virtue is exhibited by a theory can serve as a heuristic for approximating ideally rational Bayesian reasoning in inferences that resemble Harman-style IBE.

(iv) However, Harman-style IBE can only serve as a reliable heuristic for probabilistic comparisons between already-generated theories, since it is not designed to ensure that the one of the generated theories is true.

(v) While this is sometimes an acceptable limitation to IBE, such as when our aim is merely to choose which theory to pursue further, a stronger form of IBE is needed to conclude that a theory is probably true.

(vi) This may largely be achieved by adding to IBE a final step, consisting of a temporally extended process of gathering more evidence and exploring alternative explanations, before accepting the relevant theory.

(vii) Furthermore, in cases where there are multiple plausible rivals to the best explaining theory, the epistemic risk involved in IBE may be alleviated by inferring only what all these theories agree on.

Taken together, these theses show how one can coherently and plausibly reconcile the kernel of truth in traditional ideas about abductive reasoning – stemming from such luminaries as Bacon, Darwin, Peirce, and Harman, among many others – with the powerful and popular Bayesian approach to scientific reasoning. The overall account may not be as simple as one might have hoped, but then again there is little reason to think that scientific reasoning is a simple matter.

References

Bacon, F. (1620). *Novum Organum, sive Indicia Vera de Interpretatione Naturae*. John Bill, London.

Baker, A. (2003). Quantitative Parsimony and Explanatory Power. *British Journal for the Philosophy of Science*, 54:245–259.

Baker, A. (2007). Occam's Razor in Science: A Case Study from Biogeography. *Biology and Philosophy*, 22:193–215.

Baker, A. (2022). Simplicity. In Zalta, E. N., editor, *Stanford Encyclopedia of Philosophy (Summer 2022 Edition)*. Metaphysics Research Lab, Stanford University. https://plato.stanford.edu/archives/sum2022/entries/simplicity/.

Barnes, E. (1995). Inference to the Loveliest Explanation. *Synthese*, 103:252–277.

Beebe, J. R. (2009). The Abductivist Reply to Skepticism. *Philosophy and Phenomenological Research*, 79:605–636.

Biggs, S. and Wilson, J. M. (2017). The a Priority of Abduction. *Philosophical Studies*, 174(3):735–758.

Bird, A. (2017). Inference to the Best Explanation, Bayesianism, and Knowledge. In McCain, K. and Poston, T., editors, *Best Explanations: New Essays on Inference to the Best Explanation*, pages 97–120. Oxford University Press, Oxford.

Boghossian, P. (2014). What Is Inference? *Philosophical Studies*, 169(1):1–18.

Bowler, P. and Morus, I. R. (2005). *Making Modern Science: A Historical Survey*. University of Chicago Press, Chicago.

Boyd, R. (1980). Scientific Realism and Naturalistic Epistemology. *PSA: Proceedings of the Biennial Meeting of the Philosophy of Science Association*, 1980:613–662.

Burgess, J. P. (1998). Occam's Razor and Scientific Method. In Schirn, M., editor, *The Philosophy of Mathematics Today*, pages 195–214. Clarendon Press, Oxford.

Cabrera, F. (2017). Can There Be a Bayesian Explanationism? On the Prospects of a Productive Partnership. *Synthese*, 194:1245–1272.

Campos, D. G. (2011). On the Distinction between Peirce's Abduction and Lipton's Inference to the Best Explanation. *Synthese*, 180:419–442.

Chakravartty, A. (2017). Scientific Realism. In Zalta, E. N., editor, *The Stanford Encyclopedia of Philosophy (Summer 2017 Edition)*. Metaphysics Research Lab, Stanford University. https://plato.stanford.edu/archives/sum2017/entries/scientific-realism/.

Clarke, D. (1992). *Descartes' Philosophy of Science*. Manchester University Press, Manchester.

Climenhaga, N. (2017a). How Explanation Guides Confirmation. *Philosophy of Science*, 84(2):359–368.

Climenhaga, N. (2017b). Inference to the Best Explanation Made Incoherent. *Journal of Philosophy*, 114(5):251–273.

Crick, F. (1988). *What Mad Pursuit*. Basic Books, New York.

Crupi, V. (2021). Confirmation. In Zalta, E. N., editor, *The Stanford Encyclopedia of Philosophy (Spring 2021 Edition)*. Metaphysics Research Lab, Stanford University. https://plato.stanford.edu/archives/spr2021/entries/confirmation/.

Darwin, C. (1962). *On the Origin of Species*. Collier, New York.

Dawes, G. W. (2013). Belief Is Not the Issue: A Defense of Inference to the Best Explanation. *Ratio*, 26:62–78.

Dawid, R., Hartmann, S., and Sprenger, J. (2015). The No Alternatives Argument. *British Journal for the Philosophy of Science*, 66:213–234.

Day, T. and Kincaid, H. (1994). Putting Inference to the Best Explanation in Its Place. *Synthese*, 98:271–295.

Dellsén, F. (2016). Explanatory Rivals and the Ultimate Argument. *Theoria*, 82:217–237.

Dellsén, F. (2017a). Abductively Robust Inference. *Analysis*, 77:20–29.

Dellsén, F. (2017b). Certainty and Explanation in Descartes' Philosophy of Science. *HOPOS: The Journal of the International Society for the History of Philosophy of Science*, 7:302–327.

Dellsén, F. (2017c). Reactionary Responses to the Bad Lot Objection. *Studies in History and Philosophy of Science*, 61:32–40.

Dellsén, F. (2017d). Realism and the Absence of Rivals. *Synthese*, 194:2427–2446.

Dellsén, F. (2018). The Heuristic Conception of Inference to the Best Explanation. *Philosophical Studies*, 175:1745–1766.

Dellsén, F. (2021). Explanatory Consolidation: From "Best" to "Good Enough." *Philosophy and Phenomenological Research*, 103:157–177.

Descartes, R. (1985/1628). Rules for the Direction of the Mind. In Cottingham, J., Stoothoff, R., and Murdoch, D., editors, *The Philosophical Writings of Descartes*, volume I, pages 7–78. Cambridge University Press, Cambridge.

Descartes, R. (1985/1644). Principles of Philosophy. In Cottingham, J., Stoothoff, R., and Murdoch, D., editors, *The Philosophical Writings of Descartes*, volume I, pages 177–291. Cambridge University Press, Cambridge.

Dirac, P. A. M. (1931). Quantised Singularities in the Electromagnetic Field. *Proceedings of the Royal Society*, 133:60–72.

Douven, I. (2006). Assertion, Knowledge, and Rational Credibility. *Philosophical Review*, 115:449–485.

Douven, I. (2013). Inference to the Best Explanation, Dutch Books, and Inaccuracy Minimisation. *Philosophical Quarterly*, 63:428–444.

Douven, I. (2017). Inference to the Best Explanation: What Is It? And Why Should We Care? In McCain, K. and Poston, T., editors, *Best Explanations: New Essays on Inference to the Best Explanation*, pages 7–24. Oxford University Press, Oxford.

Douven, I. (2021). Abduction. In Zalta, E. N., editor, *Stanford Encyclopedia of Philosophy (Summer 2021 Edition)*. Metaphysics Research Lab, Stanford University. https://plato.stanford.edu/archives/sum2021/entries/abduction/.

Douven, I. (2022). *The Art of Abduction*. MIT Press, Cambridge, MA.

Douven, I. and Wenmackers, S. (2017). Inference to the Best Explanation versus Bayes's Rule in a Social Setting. *British Journal for the Philosophy of Science*, 68:535–570.

Earman, J. (1992). *Bayes or Bust: A Critical Examination of Bayesian Confirmation Theory*. MIT Press, Cambridge, MA.

Easwaran, K. (2011). Bayesianism II: Applications and Criticisms. *Philosophy Compass*, 6:321–332.

Egg, M. (2016). Expanding Our Grasp: Causal Knowledge and the Problem of Unconceived Alternatives. *British Journal for the Philosophy of Science*, 67:115–141.

Elliott, K. (2021). Inference to the Best Explanation and the New Size Elitism. *Philosophical Perspectives*, 35:170–188.

Fisher, R. A. (1959). *Smoking: The Cancer Controversy; Some Attempts to Assess the Evidence*. Oliver and Boyd, Edinburgh.

Foley, R. (1992). The Epistemology of Belief and the Epistemology of Degrees of Belief. *American Philosophical Quarterly*, 29:111–124.

Foster, J. (1982). Induction, Explanation, and Natural Necessity. *Proceedings of the Aristotelian Society*, 101:145–161.

Frege, G. (1979). *Posthumous Writings*. University of Chicago Press, Chicago, IL.

Fumerton, R. (1995). *Metaepistemology and Skepticism*. Rowman & Littlefield, Lanham, MD.

Galileo, G. (1962/1632). *Dialogues Concerning the Two Chief Worlds Systems*. University of Berkeley Press, Berkeley, CA.

Gigerenzer, G. (2000). *Adaptive Thinking: Rationality in the Real World*. Oxford University Press, Oxford.

Hanson, R. N. (1958). *Patterns of Discovery*. Cambridge University Press, Cambridge.

Harman, G. (1965). The Inference to the Best Explanation. *The Philosophical Review*, 74:88–95.

Harman, G. (1989). *Change in View: Principles of Reasoning*. MIT Press, Cambridge, MA.

Harman, G. (1997). Pragmatism and Reasons for Belief. In Kulp, C. B., editor, *Realism/Antirealism and Epistemology*, pages 93–116. Rowman and Littlefield, Lanham, MD.

Hempel, C. (1945). Studies in the Logic of Confirmation I & II. *Mind*, 54:1–26 & 97–121.

Hempel, C. G. (1966). *Philosophy of Natural Science*. Prentice-Hall, Englewood Cliffs, NJ.

Henderson, L. (2014). Bayesianism and Inference to the Best Explanation. *British Journal for the Philosophy of Science*, 65:687–715.

Henderson, L. (2017). Bayesianism and IBE: The Case of Individual vs. Group Selection. In McCain, K. and Poston, T., editors, *Best Explanations: New Essays on Inference to the Best Explanation*, pages 248–261. Oxford University Press, Oxford.

Henderson, L. (2022). Putting Inference to the Best Explanation into Context. *Studies in History and Philosophy of Science Part A*, 94:167–176.

Horwich, P. (1982). *Probability and Evidence*. Cambridge University Press, Cambridge.

Huemer, M. (2009). Explanationist Aid for the Theory of Inductive Logic. *British Journal for the Philosophy of Science*, 60:345–375.

Jackson, E. and Tan, P. (2022). Epistemic Akrasia and Belief-Credence Dualism. *Philosophy and Phenomenological Research*, 104:717–727.

Jansson, L. and Tallant, J. (2017). Quantative Parsimony: Probably for the Better. *British Journal for the Philosophy of Science*, 68:781–803.

Kahneman, D. (2011). *Thinking, Fast and Slow*. Farrar, Straus and Giroux, New York.

Kahneman, D., Slovic, P., and Tversky, A., editors (1982). *Judgment under Uncertainty: Heuristics and Biases*. Cambridge University Press, Cambridge.

Kapitan, T. (1992). Peirce and the Autonomy of Abductive Reasoning. *Erkenntnis*, 37:1–26.

Kashyap, A. (2023). General Relativity, MOND, and the Problem of Unconceived Alternatives. *European Journal for Philosophy of Science*, 13:30.

Keil, F. C. (2006). Explanation and Understanding. *Annual Review of Psychology*, 57:227–254.

Khalifa, K. (2010). Default Privilege and Bad Lots: Underconsideration and Explanatory Inference. *International Studies in the Philosophy of Science*, 24:91–105.

Kuhn, T. S. (1977). Objectivity, Value Judgments, and Theory Choice. In *The Essential Tension*, pages 320–339. University of Chicago Press, Chicago, IL.

Kuipers, T. (2000). *From Instrumentalism to Constructive Empiricism*. Springer, Dordrecht.

Lange, M. (2017). The Evidential Relevance of Explanatoriness: A Reply to Roche and Sober. *Analysis*, 77:303–312.

Lange, M. (2020). What Inference to the Best Explanation Is Not: A Response to Roche and Sober's Screening-Off Challenge to IBE. *Teorema: International Journal of Philosophy*, 39:27–42.

Lange, M. (2022). Putting Explanation Back Into "Inference to the Best Explanation." *Noûs*, 56:84–109.

Lange, M. (2023). A False Dichotomy in Denying Explanatoriness Any Role in Confirmation. *Noûs*, forthcoming.

Laudan, L. (1984). *Science and Values*. University of California Press, Berkeley, CA.

Lavoisier, A. (1862). *Oeuvres*. Imprimerie Impériale, Paris.

Lewis, D. (1973). *Counterfactuals*. Blackwell, Oxford.

Lipton, P. (1991). *Inference to the Best Explanation*. Routledge, London.

Lipton, P. (1993). Is the Best Good Enough? *Proceedings of the Aristotelian Society*, 93:89–104.

Lipton, P. (2001). Is Explanation a Guide to Inference? A Reply to Wesley Salmon. In Hon, G. and Rakover, S., editors, *Explanation: Theoretical Approaches and Applications*, pages 93–120. Kluwer Academic, Dordrecht.

Lipton, P. (2004). *Inference to the Best Explanation*. Routledge, London, 2nd edition.

Lombrozo, T. (2010). Explanation and Abductive Reasoning. In Holyoak, K. and Morrison, R., editors, *The Oxford Handbook of Thinking and Reasoning*, pages 260–276. Oxford University Press, Oxford.

Lycan, W. G. (1985). Epistemic Value. *Synthese*, 64:137–164.

Lycan, W. G. (1988). *Judgment and Justification*. Cambridge University Press, Cambridge.

Lycan, W. G. (2012). Explanationist Rebuttals (Coherentism Defended Again). *The Southern Journal of Philosophy*, 50:5–20.

Mackonis, A. (2011). Inference to the Best Explanation, Coherence and Other Explanatory Virtues. *Synthese*, 190:975–995.

Magnus, P. (2010). Inductions, Red Herrings, and the Best Explanation for the Mixed Records of Science. *British Journal for the Philosophy of Science*, 61:803–819.

McCain, K. and Moretti, L. (2022). *Appearance and Explanation*. Oxford University Press, Oxford.

McCain, K. and Poston, T. (2014). Why Explanatoriness Is Evidentially Relevant. *Thought*, 3:145–153.

McCain, K. and Poston, T. (2018). The Evidential Impact of Explanatory Considerations. In McCain, K. and Poston, T., editors, *Best Explanations: New Essays on Inference to the Best Explanation*, pages 121–129. Oxford University Press, Oxford.

McCain, K. and Poston, T. (2019). Dispelling the Disjunction Objection to Explanatory Inference. *Philosopher's Imprint*, 19(36):1–8.

McGrew, T. (2003). Confirmation, Heuristics, and Explanatory Reasoning. *British Journal for the Philosophy of Science*, 54:553–567.

McMullin, E. (1987). Explanatory Success and the Truth of Theory. In Rescher, N., editor, *Scientific Inquiry in Philosophical Perspective*, pages 51–73. University Press of America, Lanham, MD.

McMullin, E. (1992). *The Inference that Makes Science*. Marquette University Press, Milwaukee, WI.

Minnameier, G. (2004). Peirce-Suit of Truth - Why Inference to the Best Explanation and Abduction Ought Not to Be Confused. *Erkenntnis*, 60:75–105.

Morreau, M. (2015). Theory Choice and Social Choice: Kuhn Vindicated. *Mind*, 124:239–262.

Musgrave, A. (1988). The Ultimate Argument for Scientific Realism. In Nola, R., editor, *Relativism and Realism in Science*, pages 229–252. Kluwer Academic, Dordrecht.

Neta, R. (2013). What Is an Inference. *Philosophical Issues*, 23(1):388–407.

Niiniluoto, I. (1999). Defending Abduction. *Philosophy of Science (Proceedings Supplement)*, 66:S436–S451.

Niiniluoto, I. (2018). *Truth-Seeking by Abduction*. Springer, Cham.

Nolan, D. (1997). Quantitative Parsimony. *British Journal for the Philosophy of Science*, 48:329–343.

Nyrup, R. (2015). How Explanatory Reasoning Justifies Pursuit: A Peircean View of IBE. *Philosophy of Science*, 82:749–760.

Okasha, S. (2000). Van Fraassen's Critique of Inference to the Best Explanation. *Studies in the History and Philosophy of Science*, 31:691–710.

Okasha, S. (2011). Theory Choice and Social Choice: Kuhn versus Arrow. *Mind*, 120:83–115.

Okasha, S. (2015). On Arrow's Theorem and Scientific Rationality: Reply to Morreau and Stegenga. *Mind*, 124:279–294.

Okasha, S. and Thébault, K. (2020). Is There a Bayesian Justification of Hypothetico-Deductive Inference? *Noûs*, 54:774–794.

Peirce, C. S. (1958). *The Collected Papers of Charles Sanders Peirce*. Harvard University Press, Cambridge, MA.

Pettigrew, R. (2021). On the Pragmatic and Epistemic Virtues of Inference to the Best Explanation. *Synthese*, 199:12407–12438.

Poston, T. (2014). *Reason and Explanation: A Defense of Explanatory Coherentism*. Palgrave Macmillan, New York.

Priest, G. (2016). Logical Disputes and the a Priori. *Logique et Analyse*, 59:347–366.

Psillos, S. (1999). *Scientific Realism: How Science Tracks Truth*. Routledge, London.

Quine, W. V. O. and Ullian, J. S. (1978). *The Web of Belief*. Random House, New York.

Roche, W. and Sober, E. (2013). Explanatoriness Is Evidentially Irrelevant, or Inference to the Best Explanation meets Bayesian Confirmation Theory. *Analysis*, 73:659–668.

Roche, W. and Sober, E. (2014). Explanatoriness and Evidence: A Reply to McCain and Poston. *Thought: A Journal of Philosophy*, 3:193–199.

Roche, W. and Sober, E. (2017). Is Explanatoriness a Guide to Confirmation? A Reply to Climenhaga. *Journal for General Philosophy of Science / Zeitschrift für Allgemeine Wissenschaftstheorie*, 48:581–590.

Roche, W. and Sober, E. (2019). Inference to the Best Explanation and the Screening-Off Challenge. *Teorema: International Journal of Philosophy*, 38:121–142.

Roush, S. (2005). *Tracking Truth: Knowledge, Evidence, and Science*. Clarendon Press, Oxford.

Rowbottom, D. P. (2019). *The Instrument of Science: Scientific Anti-realism Revitalised*. Routledge, London.

Ruhmkorff, S. (2011). Some Difficulties for the Problem of Unconceived Alternatives. *Philosophy of Science*, 78:875–886.

Salmon, W. C. (1990). Rationality and Objectivity in Science, or Tom Kuhn Meets Tom Bayes. In Savage, W., editor, *Minnesota Studies in the Philosophy of Science*, Volume 14, pages 175–204. Minnesota University Press, Minneapolis, MN.

Salmon, W. C. (2001). Explanation and Confirmation: A Bayesian Critique of Inference to the Best Explanation. In Hon, G. and Rakover, S. S., editors, *Explanation: Theoretical Approaches and Applications*, pages 61–91. Springer, Dordrecht.

Sankey, H. (2008). Scientific Method. In Psillos, S. and Curd, M., editors, *The Routledge Companion to Philosophy of Science*, pages 248–258. Routledge, London.

Schickore, J. (2022). Scientific Discovery. In Zalta, E. N. and Nodelman, U., editors, *The Stanford Encyclopedia of Philosophy (Winter 2022 Edition)*. Metaphysics Research Lab, Stanford University. https://plato.stanford.edu/ archives/win2022/entries/scientific-discovery/.

Schindler, S. (2018). *Theoretical Virtues in Science*. Cambridge University Press, Cambridge.

Schupbach, J. N. (2014). Is the Bad Lot Objection Just Misguided? *Erkenntnis*, 79:55–64.

Schupbach, J. N. (2022). *Bayesianism and Scientific Reasoning*. Cambridge Elements in the Philosophy of Science. Cambridge University Press, Cambridge.

Shaffer, M. J. (2021). Van Fraassen's Best of a Bad Lot Objection, IBE and Rationality. *Logique Et Analyse*, 255:267–273.

Shimony, A. (1970). Scientific Inference. In Colodny, R. G., editor, *The Nature and Function of Scientific Theories*, pages 79–172. University of Pittsburgh Press, Pittsburgh, PA.

Sklar, L. (1981). Do Unborn Hypotheses Have Rights? *Pacific Philosophical Quarterly*, 62:17–29.

Smithson, R. (2017). The Principle of Indifference and Inductive Scepticism. *British Journal for the Philosophy of Science*, 68:253–272.

Sober, E. (1994). Let's Razor Ockham's Razor. In *From a Biological Point of View*, pages 136–157. Cambridge University Press, Cambridge.

Sober, E. (2015). *Ockham's Razors: A User's Manual*. Cambridge University Press, Cambridge.

Stanford, P. K. (2006). *Exceeding Our Grasp: Science, History, and the Problem of Unconceived Alternatives*. Oxford University Press, Oxford.

Stegenga, J. (2015). Theory Choice and Social Choice: Okasha versus Sen. *Mind*, 124:263–277.

Strevens, M. (2000). Do Large Probabilities Explain Better? *Philosophy of Science*, 67:366–390.

Swinburne, R. (1997). *Simplicity as Evidence for Truth*. Marquette University Press, Milwaukee, WI.

Thagard, P. R. (1978). The Best Explanation: Criteria for Theory Choice. *The Journal of Philosophy*, 75:76–92.

van Fraassen, B. C. (1980). *The Scientific Image*. Clarendon, Oxford.

van Fraassen, B. C. (1984). Belief and the Will. *Journal of Philosophy*, 81:235–256.

van Fraassen, B. C. (1989). *Laws and Symmetry*. Clarendon Press, Oxford.

van Fraassen, B. C. (2000). The False Hopes of Traditional Epistemology. *Philosophy and Phenomenological Research*, 60:253–280.

van Fraassen, B. C. (2002). *The Empirical Stance*. Yale University Press, New Haven, CT.

van Fraassen, B. C. (2007). From a View of Science to a New Empiricism. In Monton, B., editor, *Images of Empiricism: Essays on Science and Stances, with a Reply from Bas C. van Fraassen*, pages 337–385. Oxford University Press, Oxford.

Vogel, J. (2005). Inference to the Best Explanation. In Craig, E., editor, *The Shorter Routledge Encyclopedia of Philosophy*. Routledge, London, pages 445–446.

Voltaire, M. (1759). *An Essay on Universal History, the Manners, and Spirit of Nations: From the Reign of Charlemaign to the Age of Lewis XIV*. J. Nourse, London.

Weintraub, R. (2013). Induction and Inference to the Best Explanation. *Philosophical Studies*, 166:203–216.

Weisberg, J. (2009). Locating IBE in the Bayesian Framework. *Synthese*, 167:125–143.

Weisberg, J. (2020). Belief in Psyontology. *Philosopher's Imprint*, 20(11):1–27.

Whewell, W. (1858). *Novum Organum Renovatum*. John W. Parker and Son, London, 3rd edition.

Williamson, T. (2016). Abductive Philosophy. *The Philosophical Forum*, 47:263–280.

Woodward, J. (2006). Some Varieties of Robustness. *Journal of Economic Methodology*, 13:219–240.

Wray, K. B. (2008). The Argument from Underconsideration as Grounds for Anti-realism. *International Studies in the Philosophy of Science*, 22:317–326.

Wray, K. B. (2011). Epistemic Privilege and the Success of Science. *Nous*, 46:375–385.

Wray, K. B. (2018). *Resisting Scientfic Realism*. Cambridge University Press, Cambridge.

Acknowledgments

I am extremely grateful for helpful feedback on earlier versions of this manuscript from Nevin Climenhaga, Marc Lange, Kevin McCain, James Norton, Mattias Skipper, Olav Vassend, and two referees for Cambridge University Press. On a more personal note, I began thinking systematically about abductive reasoning when my first daughter Katrín was still a toddler; her insatiable desire to have things thoroughly explained to her has been an inspiration ever since.

Cambridge Elements ☰

Philosophy of Science

Jacob Stegenga
University of Cambridge

Jacob Stegenga is a Reader in the Department of History and Philosophy of Science at the University of Cambridge. He has published widely on fundamental topics in reasoning and rationality and philosophical problems in medicine and biology. Prior to joining Cambridge he taught in the United States and Canada, and he received his PhD from the University of California San Diego.

About the Series

This series of Elements in Philosophy of Science provides an extensive overview of the themes, topics and debates which constitute the philosophy of science. Distinguished specialists provide an up-to-date summary of the results of current research on their topics, as well as offering their own take on those topics and drawing original conclusions.

Cambridge Elements ⁼

Philosophy of Science

Printed in the United States
by Baker & Taylor Publisher Services